LIKE IT WAS YESTERDAY

To Sandy,
Never forget 9/11.

LIKE IT WAS YESTERDAY

A Journalist's Files Since 9/11

Jill Cueni-Cohen

Love,
Jill Cueni-Cohen

Legacy Road Communications
Pittsburgh, Pennsylvania

ISBN: 978-0-9764729-1-9

Produced by: Legacy Road Communications, LLC

DEDICATION

I DEDICATE THIS BOOK to the nearly 3,000 people who lost their lives on September 11, 2001. In addition, I dedicate this book to the 343 FDNY, 23 NYPD, and 37 PAPD first responders who also died trying to save others. Thanks to them, more than 10,000 occupants of both towers were saved before the towers fell, taking the lives of so many victims in the collapse. I further dedicate this book to those 92 firefighters who were lost after 9/11 (as of 2015) due to WTC-related cancer. Americans must never forget the sacrifices those heroes made that day, as well as those who continue sacrificing their own safety to protect our country. God bless America.

Foreword

Part of what you're about to read is the unfiltered reaction to the events of September 11, 2001, by one unique journalist. It is the daybook Jill kept during the day of and the days after the most horrific crime ever committed on American soil. She even does her best to remember what life was like on September 10th.

You're asking yourself, Do we need to go through this again? As her editor as well as her friend, I asked myself that question before I took on the project. It didn't take long to realize the answer is yes. This is history; personal history, to be sure, but that's the best kind. Historians writing from a safe distance of time and space do not provide gut reactions. Jill does.

She writes about her then-husband, her children, her mother, her siblings, her friends, her children's teachers, and her neighbors and the solidarity that grows from shared hardship. And she writes about New York City, where she once lived, and how deeply she felt its wounds.

Did some of what she wrote not pan out? Sure, but that was also true for other members of the news media, along with the rest of us. I made the call, along with Jill, to leave them alone. In the middle of chaos, you're going to get things wrong because events are in flux. Besides, it might help you remember what *you* got wrong. (You can also marvel at all she got right.)

Some changes in the diary were necessary solely for the purpose of clarification. Her first reference to Stefan, her then-husband, was just "Stef." I added identifiers because, at that point, she wasn't writing this for you. She was writing to make sense in her own head of a world that had undergone a wrenching change.

Jill and the rest of us had to keep adjusting our perceptions. For one thing, the total number of victims kept fluctuating. At the outset, I remember hearing it could be as many as 10,000. Then the grisly box score was repeatedly revised, but at least it was revised downward. Because nobody really knew.

Jill writes about being nervous at the sound and sight of airplanes flying over her house in the days following the attacks. I saw the lady who lived across the street from me also looking skyward fearfully. We needn't have worried, at least not initially; all commercial air traffic would be grounded nationwide for three days afterward. Those were U.S. military aircraft flying in and out of (and I'm not making this up) the 911th Airlift Wing at Pittsburgh International Airport. Once commercial flights resumed, we all were staring worriedly at contrails.

Part of the panic of that time was not knowing the why of what had happened. We need to be reminded of that. Yes, history can be written from a safe remove, and quite well, too.

But it has to be lived first.

Jay Speyerer
January, 2015

AUTHOR'S INTRODUCTION

IN THE AFTERMATH OF 9/11, the American people demonstrated a renewed interest in patriotism. However, as time goes by, people seem to have forgotten what life was like in the days before, during and just after one of the most horrific terrorist acts ever committed on US soil—right in front of our eyes.

I, too, had pretty much forgotten about the way the world had changed in an instant… and then more life-altering changes unfolded as the weeks turned into months and the months turned into years. Now we're seeing people who were babies in 2001 entering high school, and we've come to accept the fact that we can watch journalists get their heads chopped off on YouTube, and the kidnapping of school girls by monsters in the Middle East could be resolved by merely "tweeting" #bringbackourgirls (even though it wasn't). Last summer, it was all the rage to have yourself filmed dumping ice water on your own head in a country-wide dare, but it still failed to wake anyone up to the fact that there are bigger problems facing our country.

The 911 Memorial Museum was dedicated on May 15th, 2014 and opened on May 21st. I visited the site on July 14th on a scheduled press trip. I planned to write about the experience as a travel piece for North Hills Monthly Magazine, one of my regular clients. But as I walked around the museum and then took my own personal tour of my favorite big city, I began to realize that what happened there had affected me on a much deeper level.

When I returned to Pittsburgh after my NYC press trip, I did a little research before writing the 9/11 museum article, and I came upon something I had written right when it happened. The file was called "badday," and it had been sitting practically forgotten in a Windows 97 file from my first laptop. When I opened it and started reading about my own reactions to the attacks as they took place, I was transported back to a time I almost preferred to forget. However, those diary entries awoke in me the realization that 9/11 has been a theme throughout my career as a journalist.

I began writing as a stringer for the Pittsburgh Post-Gazette in October of 2001, and many of my assignments reflected on the way 9/11 was changing our lives. Boys were inspired to become soldiers, and school children did what they could to make those soldiers feel valued. As the war in Iraq raged on, some of those soldiers died; and some of them came back altered, and I was honored to write newspaper articles that would let my neighbors know what they were going through… and how we could help.

My freelance career blossomed, and I began writing for other publications around town. Every now and then the subject of 9/11 came up as people struggled to honor the victims and pursue the new post-9/11 reality.

All of this came flooding back to me as I wrote the article about the 9/11 Museum in September of 2014. A month later, on November 3, 2014, One World Trade Center – a.k.a. Freedom Tower – opened for business. This was the same day my article went live, and the coincidence convinced me that I should do more than write another article; I should put a book together. I should remind people about what we've been through since those attacks shattered our peace and sparked the War on Terrorism.

I searched my computer and easily found dozens of applicable articles that strengthened my resolve. A month later, I told my cousin Gary about my idea to write a book that chronicles the way 9/11 has affected our lives since it happened, and he told me the most amazing story. In fact, I was shocked to hear about his unique experience on 9/11 and the way it has affected all of us.

Now as the fifteenth anniversary of 9/11 approaches, along with my milestone birthday of 50, I suddenly grasp the importance of teaching those who don't or can't remember. Or even *remember* to remember. People born right before, during and after 9/11/2001 were robbed of the freedoms we used to take for granted. It was hard-fought for by our fathers, grandfathers and great-grandfathers, but by the time we reached the 21st Century, we believed we had evolved above brutal war and senseless killing. On 9/11, we found out that we were indeed still vulnerable, and it changed us.

Air travel has changed the most. Now we are all under suspicion of a seemingly tyrannical TSA. Gone are the days when you could meet people at the gate and bring a bottle of water through security. Those liberties have been eroded bit by bit, and we largely accept it in the name of safety. But the terrorists strike regardless. Shoe bomber, underwear bomber, Boston bombers. It's a greater power that limits their destruction, and our government pretends they were powerless despite warnings that these people were planning to strike.

Like It Was Yesterday is a compilation of unpublished and re-edited published material about the effects of 9/11 since the attack took place. It's a reminder for those of us who were adults in 2001; and for everyone else, it's a real-life account of how America's freedom has been gradually diminished since then.

This is indeed a history book. It chronicles how September the eleventh affected my life and the lives of my fellow countrymen. It's a book about life going on after September 12th.

The 9/11 Diary

Tuesday, September 11, 2001
8:13 PM

EVERYTHING HAS CHANGED, and we will never be the same again. Today the World Trade Center was attacked and destroyed by two jet airplanes full of regular people. The plane had been hijacked. Twenty minutes later the Pentagon was hit by another plane, and even as I write this, one of its sides is still burning and has completely caved in.

After the shock of seeing the Twin Towers smash into the streets of Lower Manhattan, I realized that my brother's office wasn't far from the scene. I tried calling his house, but I couldn't get through. The phone lines were clogged with calls from people like me, searching for our loved ones in the smoldering city. I ran to my neighbor's house, and she offered me lunch, but I told her there was no way I could eat. I just wanted to find my brother. So she gave me her phone and told me to go to it. After a few tries, I finally got through to his answering machine, where I left a message.

Then I was finally able to get through to his office's automated answering service. "Welcome to Chase, where the right relationship is everything!" announced the automated bank teller in a cheerful voice. I took comfort in the fact that the phones were working there and punched in his extension, but only managed to reach his voice mail. "Andy! Please call me and let me know you're okay!"

At noon, he left a message that was full of sorrow. He could barely speak, and I could hear him crying as he told me that his building was being evacuated and I should call him later at home. I fell apart when I heard him weeping and sounding like a scared little boy, but later he told me that he had been the one with the calm exterior, and that everybody came to him for information. He was cradling one older gentleman in his arms just to keep the guy from freaking out.

He told me that as soon as the first plane hit, everyone wanted to go out and see, but Andy blocked the door and told them that they would be leaving over his dead body. One man had actually escaped into another part of the building, and when he came back, Andy said he nearly throttled him.

They thought that a building's incinerator had exploded, and when they looked out the window, they saw pieces of paper flying through the air. Out on the street, one of their co-workers was just entering the building when he noticed a twenty-dollar bill floating down from the sky. He nudged the woman next to him, "Look! It's a twenty!" and he grabbed it out of the air, but when he looked at it, he noticed that it was covered with blood, and he dropped it on the ground and ran into the building...

Is this making any sense? I write what my brother told me when he finally got to his house on Long Island, covered in asbestos and ashes. He'd had to walk about five miles to find an operating train. He told me that the ground was littered with women's shoes.

I can't even comprehend what has happened. The television is going apeshit with grisly pictures that surely can't be real -- it's like something out of Hollywood. I'm walking around like a zombie, my eyes red and swollen, and I'm constantly on the verge of tears.

Today I cried on Laura Mitnick, and I don't even really know her! What has happened to our country? Who has committed this unspeakable crime? I felt like shaking the people in the stores with their cheerful good mornings! This was not a good morning -- in fact, it was probably the worst morning I've ever seen in all of my 36 years.

Wednesday, September 12, 2001

Went to bed early last night with the television droning endlessly about the day's terrible tragedy. The last thing I remember of Tuesday, September 11th, was Republicans and Democrats singing the National Anthem together, and then I fell into a deep, dreamless sleep, my eyes finally able to rest after all the sobbing I'd been doing since 8:50 in the morning.

Today I woke with a start, practically shouting, "What the hell?!" I guess I was hoping that yesterday was a nightmare. When I turned on the television, the scene was grisly: thousands of people digging about in the rubble that used to be the World Trade Center, dodging the other buildings that were suddenly collapsing all around them as they searched desperately for signs of life. In Washington, the fire still burns, and it's not likely that anyone has survived, but we still hold out hope...

This was a day of shock, fear, anger, sadness, despair, uncertainty, rage, confusion, understanding and pride. I dissolved into tears every time I was confronted with another account of courage in the face of terror.

I had to drive Jennifer to school because she missed the bus. As we pulled out of the driveway, the classic rock station I usually listen to began playing the National Anthem, making it hard to see the road through the tears I was trying to hide from my child. She's frightened enough as it is. I'm just glad she's spending her days in school and not around me because I am not doing very well at keeping it together. I am so grateful to her teachers for staying quiet about the attack and not letting the children know a thing. They left it up to us to tell them, which I think was the right thing to do.

Some people ran to the school right after the fourth plane went down in nearby Somerset County and picked up their children, despite disapproval from the school's psychologist. Okay, I admit I ran there too, after the rabbi closed down the temple and sent all the preschool children home. But when the elementary school's secretary assured me that the children weren't going to be told anything about it, I decided that what Jenny didn't know couldn't hurt her.

Now I wonder if that was crazy, knowing that they'd evacuated Downtown Pittsburgh, closed all the universities and even shut down the malls. When Stacey called from Bethesda, Maryland, she told me that they made all the parents come and pick up their kids from school. They were even on the brink of planning a retreat two hours away to their property on the Mason-Dixon Line, until I told her that a fourth plane had gone down in Somerset, which is a mere 20 minutes away from her plot of land in Deep Creek. It felt like there was nowhere to run, nowhere to hide.

The phone has continued to ring with calls from my family and friends in Basel, Switzerland, as well as a couple of calls from some other ex-Baslers who now live in Australia. We greatly appreciate the concern and support, but we were surprised by it until I found the BBC on TV and heard them telling the world that Pittsburgh was also attacked. Somerset is over an hour away from the 'Burgh -- it's home to our local ski resorts, Hidden Valley and Seven Springs. We're untouched by it in Pittsburgh, but they're making it look like we've been hit just like Washington and New York City. It's simply not true.

Thursday, September 13, 2001
8:46 AM

I keep telling all the folks in Switzerland that we're safe in Pittsburgh on Tuesday, and now I learn that the doomed flight could just as easily have hit our USX (U.S. Steel) tower as passengers fought for control of the plane right above our heads. Some of the moms from the temple even saw a plane flying low and erratically at just about the same time.

Pittsburgh, New York and Washington -- there's someone I love in every city that was airplane bombed, and I'm telling the Swiss and the Aussies that we're all right. We're *not* all right. That airplane crashed in what just might as well be our own backyard, and they're talking about Pittsburgh because it happened in the airspace over Pittsburgh. It was by the grace of God that it landed in an empty field instead of killing masses and destroying buildings, decimating skylines.

God, they've dismembered the coveted NYC skyline -- it doesn't even seem real. It's like we're marching about in this bizarre, morbid, angry movie. They're pulling bodies out of the wreckage -- well, not even bodies -- body parts. Miraculously, six firemen have come out of the rubble alive. I believe there are more to be found, but they must work quickly to free them...

How do I prepare for World War III? Will I survive it? Quitting my bad habits seems pointless now. Did the woman who'd just lost 25 pounds have time to grab a donut before plunging to her death from the 103rd floor of Tower One? Did Joe Shmo, who quit smoking for a year, wish he could have had one last puff before the fire took his skin off? What does it matter when it could all be over in an instant of impact and we're lost beneath the rubble of WAR and HATE? DEATH and DESTRUCTION! Fighting for a return to Monday's peaceful freedom, the day before all hell broke loose.

What did I even do on Monday, September 10th? It was actually a really happy day for me: Toby started his first day of preschool, and my mom took me out to breakfast to celebrate. Later that day, I transcribed a huge pile of letters from the days of yore, so excited about preparing to finish my book with known information -- and all I have to do is compile it all into the last third of the story: The New York Chronicles.

I hear motor sounds in the distance and wonder if it's a plane or a helicopter. I've been running outside and peering at the sky for the past three days the moment I hear that telltale roar in the sky. I've always looked at planes in dread that I might watch one blow up, and I always imagined the Twin Towers falling, but I never put the two together.

It's raining outside, and lightning just struck. I'm glad it's not an airplane crashing into the USX Tower, but I'm worried anyway. However, I'm learning that disaster happens on clear, sunny days, so I suppose we're safer in a stormy night, despite the dangers of lightning. Oh great, now I think I hear a chopper. Will the war that started here be fought on foreign soil? Our country continues to be threatened by the unknown cowards who so badly want us to feel the pain and devastation of war in our own country for once. Well, we fucking hate it, too, assholes, so why don't you just STOP THE KILLING! STOP THE DESTRUCTION!

Our people are calling for it, too. BOMB AFGHANISTAN! SLAUGHTER THE ARAB BASTARDS! DEATH TO ISLAMIC FUNDAMENTALISTS! They're hoping we'll sink to their level. I mean, where will it end? Do we have to destroy each other in order to be reborn as a peaceful world?

Every time I've gotten on a plane since I've had children, I've prepared for the possibility that it could be the last thing we ever do. Every trip, from Switzerland to New York and back again, has been a risk I've taken. I've always considered that risk and weighed it against the way I've always lived my life -- to the fullest right up until the end.

Every planeload of passengers and crew I've traveled with has been under my scrutiny as I took my seat and wondered if we'd all become famous together or be allowed to go our own separate ways after the flight has ended and we got our luggage and left without a backward glance at any one person, unless chance throws us together in the same place at the same time again.

Meetings on airplanes

I once met a very attractive businessman on a flight from New York to Columbus, Ohio. I gave him my phone number, because back then, I gave out my phone number on occasion. Well, this guy even called me, but that's all that ever came of it, because I was learning to be distrustful of men, and I didn't know anything about him.

My last journey home to Switzerland, I knew quite a few people on the flight, and it was the best international trip ever. It was the first time I didn't cry on an eastward-bound airplane.

I've seen great acts of kindness on airplanes -- people were always happy to help the young mother juggle an infant, a toddler and a little dog from Zürich to Dulles International Airport and on into Pittsburgh.

It was "Curriculum Night" at Jennifer's school tonight. The parents enthusiastically applauded the teachers for masking their emotions on Tuesday and staying calm in the face of disaster. I asked Jenn's second grade teacher how he pulled it off, and he sighed before admitting that it was very difficult.

My daughter told me that he got the news while he was in front of the class, but that he acted business-as-usual. Jennifer came home that day, happily skipping off the school bus without a care in the world, and I had to shatter it with my horrific news. She was frightened until she spent the day in school yesterday, claiming that Mr. Piper didn't really say anything about it.

It was kind of nice to forget about disaster for a couple of hours as I turned my attention towards the people who are going to help mold my child into a literate American. We even had a good laugh when a new teacher, fresh from the university, was explaining that the kids were going to get "whoops slips" every time they forget their homework. I raised my hand and asked if I should drop off forgotten homework and spare my daughter the dreaded notification or if I should just let her suffer the consequences. "Well," admitted the young woman, "I forgot something I needed for tonight, and I had to call my mother to come and bring it to me."

Friday, September 14, 2001

Today was a day of prayer. A bunch of my neighbors collected on the street in front of our houses and participated in the countrywide candlelight vigil at 7:00 p.m. We were nine adults, five children and one dog, standing in front of our homes, dripping wax and trying to sing songs we don't even know all the words to. We tried to have a moment of silence, but that proved impossible with five children who have never even heard the old adage that they should be seen and not heard. We didn't get even five seconds of silence, but it was still a good feeling to be together at this time of strife. Then we all piled into the car and headed for the synagogue for Sabbath services.

Sunday, September 16, 2001

Must force myself to write these days, and it's so hard. Felt the need to go to Somerset today, so at 4:00 the whole family piled into the car and set off for the crash site, just an hour and a half away. We couldn't get too close because roads were closed, and we could only see cranes in the distance behind a yellow police line tape. There was some metal debris directly behind the police line, but it could also have been mere garbage on the side of the road. Macabre.

Five-year-old Toby heard on the radio that they need blood donations. "Why don't they just use the blood from the people who died? They sure don't need it anymore."

I ask my [Swiss] husband, Stefan, "What do you think about life now?"

"I think life is in the family, and you should not look for more and more and be greedy. You should look for family issues."

"But didn't you always think like this?"

"Yeah. Basically, yes."

"So what's changed?"

"I don't know. A lot. A big switch got turned on in my brain since this happened. Like don't wait for things that might happen in the future, or what you will do in the future, but think right now what you can do to improve yourself and other people's quality of life. You know how we always run for goals and play the lottery and think how we could win? Well, it's important to have goals and hopes, but don't let your daily life get run by these thoughts."

On the evening of September 11th, Stef and I stood there in the basement while the kids were upstairs watching Nickelodeon, one of the only unaffected television stations, and we listened to the president speak to us, with conviction and great strength, but also great sadness. "God Bless America," he told us, and we held on tightly to one another and just cried together, like never before.

I've been chewing my cuticles so much my fingers are like dog meat.

Stef wonders how the people in Africa filming Survivor must feel -- if they're even there now. I wonder if they would tell them.

"Has your opinion of America changed?" I ask my husband, who hasn't been digging being here all that much in the first place.

"Yes, totally. Seeing people really standing together, putting flags out, lighting candles -- in a country that's so big -- that impressed me."

"What did you think about us before this?"

"Like a nice facade, but everybody was just running by themselves to make their lives as good as possible no matter what the cost is."

I want to write an article for *Hello, Basel* magazine. I could donate the fee to the relief fund.

Tuesday, September 11th, had been a clear, sunny day. I had just come back in the house after taking Jennifer to the bus stop and chatting with my neighbors for a few minutes after the bus had gone. I rushed back into the house at about 8:50 to get Toby ready for his second day of preschool. I had tentative plans to drive out to Beaver to visit with my buddy Moe, but after spending the night before, working on my novel 'til the wee hours of the morning, I called her to tell her that I wouldn't make it, and she says, "Turn on the television! An airplane just crashed into the World Trade Center!"

By the time I'd made it upstairs and turned on the set in our bedroom, Stef was just getting out of the shower, and the television was sporting a horrific scene.

Stef says, "I was really impressed with how these companies donated money -- like Cisco, which has been having problems on the stock market, but they donated five million."

Monday, September 17, 2001

Life is slowly getting back to "normal," but it seems absurd. We're in this crazy holding pattern, and it's almost ridiculous to hear ads for companies like Travelocity that urge you to plan NOW for your vacation, that the prices are GREAT! United announced today that it plans on laying off 11,000 employees. Continental might declare bankruptcy, and one small airline folded the day after the disaster. It's become so inconvenient to fly now, not to mention scary, that everyone's decided to either postpone their far away trips or take another form of transportation.

My husband and I have discussed our plans for escape, in the event that things get downright dangerous -- like a nuclear bomb or constant terrorist acts happening all around us. We don't want to even think about the grim possibilities, but when you see some of the most important buildings of our country burning with the fire of hatred, drenched in jet fuel and people jumping out of the windows into angels' waiting wings, it is not inconceivable that we may need to flee under cover of our Swiss Citizenship.

Tuesday, September 18, 2001

FEAR

Tornadoes are swirling funnel clouds of destruction like a huge Hoover in the sky, but with no bag to catch the debris. It just twists around in the vortex until it is thrown to the winds of fate. Tornadoes terrified me as a child, when I decided that they were the evil hand of an angry force we could not see, dipping into our atmosphere and stirring up trouble. I am fascinated and frightened by their force. Talk about unseen enemies.

Images of planes flying into the buildings that signify the gateway to freedom in a city I have lived in and still love are never far from my mind. The figure of a person waving a white cloth from the edge of the gaping hole in Tower One, and knowing that he had plunged to his death when the building collapsed around him and into itself, like a deck of cards, shoving the victims so far down into its vortex, that it's been just over a week and they still haven't found the majority of the 5000+ people who have been reported missing since the disaster.

There is a wall in the city that is covered with the images of these people in happy times, getting married, holding babies, hugging dogs... Smiling mug shots of a time when they had no reason to fear going to work. Children have been orphaned, pets have been abandoned, leases broken, weddings called off, lives shattered....

Jobs lost. US Airways plans on laying off 20,000 employees.

A city in ruins. Buildings stand precariously, awaiting demolition, maybe sooner rather than later. Fires still burn in places, and a tower of smoke is imitating the missing WTC. My friend Jersey Jeff thinks the Twin Towers should be rebuilt, stronger and taller than before, but who would want to work there?

Confidence lost. The stock market opened up yesterday, amidst the asbestos that blankets Lower Manhattan and rises like a menacing mist. To everyone's dismay, it plummeted 850 points, and my stock broker neighbors came home with grim faces, muttering that it could have been worse...

Today it leveled off, and the Fed dropped the interest rate half a percent to stimulate the market. Still, there was only a handful of people at the Pirates game tonight. Nobody really wants to go out and enjoy themselves these days, when the threat of war looms dark and bloody in the uncertain future.

I flick on the television the moment my eyes open. Keep seeing the President in press conference after press conference, warning us that the fight will be long and arduous, and at the same time he tries to encourage us to go out and spend money, get back to the business of living like we did before, but we all know that's impossible.

Nothing will ever be the same again. We have been chastened harshly for ignoring the warning signs: the bombs that destroyed our embassies and the airplane that exploded off the coast of Long Island for no apparent reason, not to mention the bombing of the WTC itself, less than eight years ago. Colin Powell looks so cool and confident and ready to kick some terrorist butt, but he preaches tolerance towards our fellow Americans of Middle Eastern decent. Yet how can we know who's good and who's bad? Their hatred is unimaginable, their determination in our destruction steadfast. They hide in the shadows and won't reveal themselves to us, and we're all at risk.

Wednesday, September 19, 2001

I'm sick of watching the towers crumble, over and over -- on fire, falling down, on fire, falling down... On Tuesday around 9:45, I watched the South Tower standing lost and lonely after the North Tower had gone down, and I knew that if I stood there long enough, I would get to witness a moment in history, via live television coverage. I felt sick and heartbroken, terrified and furious, all at the same time while I considered the countless innocent office workers who were being pulverized with the force of 110 floors crashing down upon them. It was a horrific scene, and watching it happen again and again is diminishing its effect.

It was awful enough to watch it live, but watching it turn into a fascination, like a scene from a Hollywood production -- I think it's desensitizing. Why are we forced to keep watching the murder of thousands of civilians, the destruction of one of America's most famous gateways? It's even being shown at North Park Lounge on the television at the bar. There's no getting away from it.

The stock market dropped 170 points today, and on top of that, a new virus has invaded computers all over the world. Even Stef was affected at Radio Shack because the main server in Texas has been infected. According to the news shows, the terrorists are everywhere, and they have been planning our destruction for a long time.

I'm learning now of terrorist plans that have been thwarted, and how the jihad is a holy war that some Islamic Muslims have been waging against us for some time, and we didn't even know it. Oh, it was alluded to in the past, but the average American didn't really take notice because it barely touched our daily lives.

Thursday, September 20, 2001

My Grandmother's not too afraid of World War Three; her brother served in World War II and her father served in World War I, so what's another war to an octogenarian who's seen it all?

Today's enemy is cunning... and crazy like a fox. They just want us dead because their people see our culture and get jealous of our freedoms. They covet our possessions and our lifestyles, especially the women. Women in Iran must live in fear. They are captive slaves who must hide themselves behind drapes of silken cloth. Lipstick is a crime, and sex is a sin.

The television is deluged with shows about the Taliban, Osama bin Laden, Islamic Fundamentalism and the ongoing dispute they have with Israel over land and laws. Just in the last few days, I've learned that Muslims pray to Mohammed, whom they believed was the second son of God. It is a religion much like Judaism, with strict dietary laws against pork.

Mirsada, my cleaning lady in Switzerland, was a Muslim. A refugee from the Bosnian War, she had no hatred for me, quite the opposite: she loves me dearly and my being an American Jew was never an issue between us. We were, instead, fascinated with each other's cultures, and we recognized similarities all the time. I can't believe that these evildoers are really Muslim or that they even pray to God. Anyone who kills and destroys with such abandon, taking their own lives in the process, has no conception of God. This is the antithesis of God. It's pure, unadulterated evil.

Now it turns out that the terrorists, in knowing that the NYSE would become incapacitated with the destruction of the World Trade Center, have bought stock options in anticipation of the resultant drop in the market. So this is the third way they plan to annihilate us: in the wallet.

President Bush gave a State of the Union address that was eloquent and full of conviction. Again, he warned of the enemy's insidious motives, telling us that they do not differentiate between civilians and soldiers, and that even women and children are considered fair game. He hinted at the threat of nuclear and biological warfare.

If there's a warning ahead of time, we plan to take a long vacation in Switzerland. There's no two ways about it, and Bunny, our miniature poodle, is coming, too.

Here's one silver lining on this dark, dangerous cloud: The dollar has gone down.

My mother-in-law is wringing her hands with worry in Switzerland. She's made it clear that we should come back if things start to get really bad. She's even offered to buy us business class tickets.

Meanwhile, Stef just said "gum-ban" just like a Pittsburgher. (Translation for Americans: a gum band is a rubber band.) He says it makes sense because the word for rubber in German is *Gummi.*

On the other hand, my mother isn't very concerned about the upcoming war. She's more worried about the tumor on one of her ovaries, even though the doctor doesn't think it's at all malignant. No, war doesn't bother her, but she doesn't like my fearful reaction, and she's very insulted by Rosmarie's questions about whether we have a nearby bomb shelter to go to. She thought it was ridiculous that Rosmarie wants to send us money to buy some food supplies, like a hundred gallons of water, just in case.

Friday, September 21, 2001

I'm sick of reporters telling us every little detail about how easy it is to infiltrate our airlines and our airports. Nightline, Dateline, 48 Hours, PBS specials... they all keep focusing on how much at risk we are, how vulnerable we are in our freedom.

I wonder, if it's so easy to attack us, why hasn't it happened before? Okay, maybe that's the wrong question, because it certainly has happened before, but how many evil plots have been thwarted? I keep hearing about a Millennium plan to destroy the festivities in Seattle with bombs, but the event proceeded peacefully and uneventfully, in Seattle and all over the world.

How stupid is it to broadcast our weaknesses to the very people who wish to do us harm? Will the Information Age bring about our undoing? Then again, consider the mighty cell phone for a moment. What a helpful invention that turned out to be. Who needs a black box recorder when every third passenger is sure to have a wireless on hand!

In the news...
There's been a shooting in Detroit of a federal agent, possibly tied to the trials of three suspects in the bombing, which was apparently taking place right across the street.

Something else that's been bothering me: KDKA News last night kept talking about "Operation Infinite Justice," which was rumored to be the code name for rooting out terrorism. However, the word Infinite has certain religious, god-like implications, and as such would be quite a provocative tone to Muslims. Infinite Justice is not the code name for the reasons I just put forth, and it was irritating to hear it said on the local news, without first being verified.

Tonight there's going to be a huge benefit concert to raise money for the victims of the disaster. Already, billions of dollars have been raised in response to the crisis, and Americans are being urged to open their wallets and donate as much as they can. Even at school today, all the kids were told to donate at least a dollar to a fund for the United Way and wear a hat to show their solidarity and patriotism.

The day after the bombing, callers on the radio morning shows kept asking that everyone put Old Glory out, and it looks like the Fourth of July in every neighborhood, every city. There are, of course, the odd house or two devoid of flags, and I find myself resenting those people who think they're too dignified to show their support in such a small yet vocal way.

I even found myself wondering about the house down the street, where I had noticed last year that an Indian family had moved in. They don't display any flags, and I can't believe the things I'm thinking about them because of it! It makes me ashamed, but I can't help feeling frightened.

The large number of planes flying over my house this afternoon has been freaking me out! It's surely not possible, but it seems like there's more planes now than ever before. And they're low-flying, too. I can often see what airline is invading my airspace as I glare at every big fat mechanical bird that passes overhead. Airplanes are totally creeping me out.

11:01 PM

The presentation of our lives has been underway for two hours now, and Willie Nelson's singing "America, the Beautiful" as the ultimate ending to an unbelievable show. No, it was more than a show. It was a collection of our country's best and brightest stars making the most creative, touching plea for an end to terrorism, an end to hate, an end to intolerance. We are a generation sobered by the reality that we are living in a world where evil is lurking. "You hoped to make a country of victims, but instead you made a country of heroes," was one message that brought home to me the fact that every generation must establish itself and do its duty to attempt to eradicate the evils that dwell in some men's souls.

Perhaps it's a rite of passage that each generation must experience a world war. Maybe it's a just a part of growing up and taking responsibility for our own generation's unique position in history.

I haven't had a really good cry in the past two days, but tonight I broke down, blubbering along with "Bridge Over Troubled Waters" and finally admitting to myself that what they've done to New York City has broken my heart. I am draining myself of tears as the concert puts names and faces on the people who perished in the attack. There was no escaping this concert: it was on every other television station, and it dominated the radio. The message of peace and of hope and of determination to put an end to hate and terrorism and reckless destruction reached out to American citizens and spread its musical wings throughout more than 60 countries around the world.

How typical of the Americans to use their creativity to let the whole world know that we cannot stand for this despicable behavior. Dan Rather started sobbing on Letterman and made them cut to commercial, but we all saw his pain, his devastation at being forced to talk about it every minute of his life.

And then there was Lisa Beamer, the wife of the man, Todd, who rolled over the terrorists with a bunch of the most courageous passengers in history. She looked positively bewildered at the unexpected turn her life has taken with the death of her husband in such a heroic way. God, I am so thankful to those dudes: all-American boys who fully grasped the desperate situation at hand and fought the very first battle of World War Three, forcing the plane down into a Pennsylvania field and sparing the lives of who knows how many. That's one of the reasons I felt compelled to pay my condolences at the crash site -- I am grateful to them beyond belief. The other reason I went was because I could.

Living in Switzerland for eight years taught me to really appreciate my American birthright. It wasn't that I hated Switzerland; quite the opposite. I learned to love my adopted homeland and felt honored when they bestowed the Swiss passport upon me. It was like I had passed the final test, and when I return to Basel as an American tourist, I'm treated like an honored guest.

Yet I spent all those years just missing America. Hearing patriotic songs has moved me to tears ever since I left my country in 1990 -- forever, or so I thought. For eight years I watched from behind the golden bars of the beautiful cage as my family carried on in life and death situations: the death of my 99-year-old great-grandmother, the time my sister fell off her horse and was in a coma for a week. There was little comfort for me, adrift from my people as I experienced grief and fear and frustration and not being able to do a thing to help because I was so damn far away, all by myself.

Maybe it was closed-minded of me, but I found my refuge in the English-speaking community of Basel, because it was my only link to the real world, where I could understand everyone and they could understand me. I appreciated my extensive education in European culture, adored meeting people from all over the globe and enjoyed living in the safe, clean, indescribably beautiful environment. But oh, how I missed my people; the spacious skies, the amber waves of grain... The ability to buy a box of Pop Tarts at 2 a.m. with a credit card, clad in sweatpants and a T-shirt.

I feel so blessed to be able to finally wear my heart upon my sleeve and cry with my neighbors, friends and family as we share our grief and outrage together. I've also found a great source of comfort within my synagogue. The first Friday after it happened, Rabbi Art invited two local ministers to our Sabbath services. The temple was packed with people from our congregation, as well as Gentiles from our community, singing God Bless America. Not a dry eye in the house after that one.

The only thing I can criticize us for is the embarrassing fact that we don't know all the words to some of our most famous American songs. We start out real strong, but when it comes time for the second verse, the whole thing peters out and we're practically whispering a jumbled version of the real thing until we get back to the verses we know. If it weren't so pathetic, it'd be comical. At least all the children have learned the actual words in school.

At last night's Flyers/Rangers hockey game in Philadelphia, they were about to start the third period when the fans began yelling to stop the game and show the President's speech. So they ended the game and watched Mr. Bush instead. Then both teams shook each other's hands and declared the game a tie. Everybody won.

Sunday, September 23, 2001
4:05 PM

God Bless Americans! Pray for us. Let freedom ring! United we stand! These are just some of the slogans written upon storefront message boards in front of many businesses in Pittsburgh. There are so many American flags being displayed that the stores have run out of them. People are even putting them on the antennas of their cars. The Fourth of July now pales in comparison to the patriotism we feel compelled to exhibit these days.

Yesterday, however, it was the only thing that reminded me of what has happened. Life has gone back to normal, or so it seems. The television was conspicuously devoid of news. It was like All-Sports Day or something. Every other channel was engaged in a football, baseball or hockey game, and only CNN and Fox News were providing updates. Not a sports fan, I turned the television off for a while, but it didn't take me long to wonder what was going on in the world of war. I never paid that much attention before, but now I think it's crucial to know what's going on with the investigation.

It's a quiet, gorgeous Sunday afternoon, but the constant air traffic overhead makes me uneasy, and I know I'm not the only one. I notice my neighbors peering into the sky at the planes -- they seem to be flying lower than they used to, and it looks like we must be under one of the busiest flight paths in Pittsburgh, because it seems like they're shattering the silence every few minutes. I'll time them while I'm writing. *(4:21 PM small, looks to be a commuter plane to the right of my house)*

On Tuesday the 11th, and two days after that, the lack of air traffic was very noticeable, and every plane and helicopter *(4:32 PM US Airways jet to the left of my house)* was of utter fascination to us all. On the news they keep telling us how easy it is to get weapons on board, even today. People keep smuggling now infamous "box cutters" and knives, even guns onto airplanes and then reporting it to the media, like we want the terrorists to know that it's possible! It makes me so angry when I see that and then have to take my brother to the Pittsburgh Airport at 9:45 a.m. to catch a flight that takes off at 12:30 -- and we thought we were cutting it close!

(4:38 PM huge jetliner right overhead, and all I could see was its underbelly)

Andy drove here yesterday with our cousin Rachel, who was moving back to Pittsburgh from Uptown Manhattan. She'd been planning this move since last summer, but I'm sure she's glad to be getting out now.

She'd rented a Ryder truck, and Andy said it was searched on their way out of the city. They're systematically searching every truck going in and out of New York City, but Andy thinks that two blond Americans were considered a low risk, and they were sent through rather quickly, but not before the agents opened the trucks and had a quick peek at the contents.

My brother's been back to work since last Thursday, and he says it's been difficult to get people to come into the city since Tuesday. The office has been relocated to another building uptown, but the fear is still keeping the people who witnessed the second plane flying into the World Trade Center in a lingering state of shock.

Five of Chase Manhattan Bank's buildings were affected by the blast, and many people are also still in shock. Two of their employees died, and many more were injured. They've got a counselor on hand, and Andy's been seeing her, too. He says he wants to talk about it all the time, but his wife, however, does not. She's doing her residency as a physician's assistant, and she's focused on that. Talk of bombs and war makes her nervous and upset, so Andy's allowed to talk about it with her for only 10 minutes a day.

(5:06 PM That one went to the right of my house, and seemed a little higher up than the others)

I'm having one good cry a day. I keep marveling at my composure, but when I think about the people whose lives will never be the same again -- the orphaned children, widowed husbands and wives, the abandoned pets, the rashes of memorial services for bodies that probably won't ever be recovered -- it takes my breath away and makes me want to sob. I read in the paper that they're asking the families and friends of victims to bring in the toothbrushes and hair brushes they used in order to do DNA testing on them in hopes of identifying the scattered remains. There are people who will never get closure.

I saw one woman on the news who had gone to Ground Zero and scooped up some ash to put in a vial to represent her "missing" sister. The media are scooping this stuff up and serving it to us daily.

Monday, September 24, 2001

At the bus stop this morning, my next-door neighbor, whose wife is a stockbroker, made this statement: "Today's the day we all get rich!" I was like, Say what? So he tells me that stocks have soared. Our stocks are still down, so we'll continue to wait for better times before selling. Stef and I think we should never dabble in the market again because it's way too risky.

At this point, about 120,000 workers have been laid off or let go. Today, however, Stef got a promotion: from managing a Radio Shack in a strip mall just off of one the ugliest highways in town to managing a Radio Shack in Northway Mall. His present store has been under renovation now that they're putting in a new Home Depot, which will be huge and not even open until February. Just after he told me about the plane going down in Somerset, he made the joke that at least they're not going to aim for where his store is because it looks like it has already been bombed.

Anyway, things are looking up for us in that department. Also, I was approached today by the woman who puts together the newsletter for our temple to take over for her in November. I'm seriously considering it.

Tomorrow it will be exactly two weeks since the attack, and it has been the longest two weeks of my life.

Monday, October 08, 2001

Yesterday our country bombed Afghanistan. Stef was glued to the television set, but I kept my distance. I don't really want to know what's going on there, just the basics, please, because I've had enough of hearing about the death of innocent people.

Andy's been sending me so many emails that my computer practically crashed from the weight of them. I don't really like receiving all this weird email where people analyze the flight numbers and manipulate them in prophetic, slightly eerie ways. Then there's the poem that reads like Dr. Seuss' *Grinch Who Stole Christmas*, and it's called The Binch.

At my book club meeting last week, one of the women was complaining that everyone's talking about that horrible man hiding out over in Afghanistan. She didn't even want to say his name because she thinks he doesn't deserve to even have one. "We should just call him 'that evil person' or something." And I agree with her. His name is now synonymous with Beelzebub. He's straight from Hell.

I celebrated Simchat Torah at the temple tonight. It was a long, joyous celebration with a string quartet and Julie Newman singing her heart out. I was praying my heart out -- praying for peace, praying for a quick end to the death and destruction.

I'm still looking at planes in the sky as flying bombs.

I haven't wanted to write until tonight. I just wanted to think I could finish with this journal of war and pretend that nothing else was going to happen. One of Andy's emails was from a guy who was from Afghanistan. He said to look at the Taliban and "that evil person" as Hitler and his regime. He said that the Muslims in Afghanistan should be looked upon as Jews in a concentration camp. It's that desperate.

It doesn't take much to set me off. Last Saturday was the Columbus Day parade in the city. Toby and I stumbled upon it and decided to have a look. I couldn't stop the tears as I watched the young majorettes march by singing Yankee Doodle Dandy and looking as if they didn't have a care in the world.

When I lived in Switzerland, I teared up every time I heard a patriotic American song, and I thought it was just homesickness. But now it's an even stronger reaction than ever before, as I try to belt out the words to The Star Spangled Banner without choking to death on my own phlegm. This morning on the radio there was a whole program devoted to the story of how Francis Scott Key wrote that song, and it was incredible how important it still is today.

I am frightened to venture out in public, I admit it, but I refuse to let them keep me from living my life like the free American woman that I am. I am terrified for the people of Afghanistan, and I am terrified for us.

Tuesday, October 16, 2001

White, powdery substance. Baking soda? Mashed potatoes? Talcum powder? What could be worse than cocaine? Or heroin? Anthrax!

One of the schools in our district has been closed since yesterday because a janitor found a white, powdery substance somewhere on the school grounds. A sample (baby formula, baking powder, saccharine?) was sent to the Center for Disease Control in Atlanta, and the children are being relocated to other schools around the district until they get the all-clear. No anthrax. Maybe it was just flour.

Fear of all white, powdery substances found in unusual places has reached a fever pitch as flights are delayed and buildings are evacuated. I have a feeling they're just trying to keep our minds off of the really scary stuff.

Wednesday, October 17, 2001

There's been this spooky email circulating that warns everyone to stay out of the malls on Halloween. Pretty stupid, considering that people are out on the streets trick-or-treating, not in the malls. The malls around here usually hold their celebrations a couple of days before the 31st. I'm not going to the mall on Halloween, but then again, I wasn't intending to anyway.

Anthrax scares closed down Congress today, and about 30 people from Senator Daschle's office have tested positive for exposure to the disease. I don't want to talk about anthrax anymore because they're shoving it down our throats all over the television and tabloids.

I heard the other day that one of the reasons they sent an anthrax letter to that office in Florida was because they housed a tabloid which had said that Osama bin Laden has a little penis. Can you imagine?

I heard tonight that the credit cards that were used to purchase the flying bomb tickets are still being used. Which means that they're still out there. The terrorists are among us. Apparently they're in New Jersey, Maryland and Florida. But it's hard to know the truth about anything.

Today the grocery check-out guy said that the media's probably getting their just desserts, and we're all watching their freaked-out coverage "so we can see how they die." Even a 7-month-old baby, who was visiting its father at the NBC office that got an anthrax letter, has been diagnosed with the cutaneous form of it.

~end of diary entries~

Articles

DOCUMENTING A DISASTER

ON THE MORNING OF SEPTEMBER 11TH, 2001, my cousin Gary, a media consultant to the Defense Logistics Agency (DLA), suddenly found himself with a unique perspective on the unfolding disaster. "My role was to collect all of the footage that had been shot by news agencies and consumer video cameras," he said, reminding me that 9/11 took place during a time when most phones and devices did not have video capabilities. Any footage shot at the time was taken by tourists with cameras and by news agencies.

In those days, Gary was on the front lines of the video revolution, and he was hired by the Pentagon to usher our armed forces into the 21st Century. "Prior to 9/11, I had done two jobs for the Pentagon. The first was making kiosks that were put in the Pentagon while they were renovating it to tell people things like where to go, areas that were under construction, how to get from point A to point B… the place is so big, so while that work was going on, it was crucial," he said, adding that he had been given security clearances to do that.

The second government contract involved something called Army Television. According to their LinkedIn page, "Army Television, a division of Army Multimedia & Visual Information Directorate (AMVID), is the preeminent television production support provider to Headquarters Department of the Army, Secretary of Defense, and other Department of Defense agencies in the National Capital Region.

"Army Television provides studio and field production, post production, audiovisual presentation services and operates the Pentagon Auditorium. In addition to Army Television, AMVID also includes: Army Photography, providing executive portraiture and historical documentation; Army Graphics, specializing in print and digital graphics products; and Production Acquisition, contracting major productions for the Department of the Army."

"They (Army Television) wanted to modernize and do digital non-linear editing like the rest of the world. They were still shooting on Betacam and ¾ inch tape," Gary recalled. He was contracted to develop the training program and was in the process of doing so. "We put the hardware chips into the military's Avid system three months before that, so the data would stay the property of the army. That was our security protocol."

Gary was on the eastern shore of Delaware, attending a meeting, when the first attacks took place in New York City. Flight 77 crashed into the western side of the Pentagon at 9:37 a.m.., and Gary received a call shortly thereafter. "We turned on the news at about 9:45, and the meeting stopped. We all watched the TV, and there were concerns about shutting down bridges like the Chesapeake Bay Bridge. Were there more planes coming out of the sky? We didn't know.

"At 10:45 we heard about Pennsylvania, and we didn't know what to expect… were there hundreds more? At 11:00, I received a call asking me to come to the Pentagon to discuss security and getting all footage (taken of the attacks), because they were declaring a state of emergency. They told me to come in—I was two and a half hours away—and they told me to contact all of the news agencies and gather that footage and bring it in.

"By noon, the first close-up footage was finally hitting the air," said Gary, adding that prior footage released on television was only wide shots of the buildings. "The news agencies were running one of the Twin Towers coming down, and you could see people jumping out of windows. Really horrific stuff, but it was just on local news agencies and not much was being shown elsewhere. By 2:00 p.m., people (government agents) were in cars, sent to the news agencies, and directed to retrieve that material. They were taking cameras from people on the street, telling them this is a national emergency. They said it was an act of terrorism, and they needed forensic evidence.

"By 3:00 p.m., they had a tap on everything. The areas around there were so inundated with smoke and dust; there wasn't much the news agencies could shoot fresh. You also couldn't get that close, because it was so dark and smoldering." Every bit of footage shot of the attack took place during a four-hour window.

Many people were going directly to the news stations with their footage but were being met by federal agents instead. "People were compensated for their cameras and film, but the government couldn't have that evidence out there. In the midst of it, people were willing to give their cameras to help," Gary recalled.

"By 6:00 p.m., most of the material had been 'sequestered,' and then we worked through the night digitizing it. The next morning, I had it all on a hard drive, and I wrote a catalogue and a report on it. By the time we trimmed it up, there were about two and a half, three hours' worth of shots taken from all the different angles."

Gary said that the images that did leak out immediately after the event were the ones of people jumping off the buildings, and most of those were shut down after one or two plays. "You could see bodies hitting the ground, and it was devastating," he recalled, adding that those images still haunt him. "As much as you can picture explosion and carnage in action films produced by the media, none of that can have the impact on you that the reality of those shots did. When a body is hitting the ground from 180 feet, it comes apart -- it splatters. It's not what you would expect it to be. It's almost impossible to even recognize what you're seeing, because you have no context for it. Your mind almost shuts off what you're looking at as a defense mechanism. You have to become methodical about what you're looking at and putting together, because you're detaching yourself from it. You almost have to sustain the disbelief that what you're looking at could actually be real."

Categorized by what agency the shots came from, what kind of camera each was taken on, what the compression was, and what the limitations were of each source, Gary's compilation was ready for him to present to the Department of Defense and the Senate on Friday.

He had pulled out frames in order to point out key moments, such as which floor the planes hit and shots of where the fuselage broke off. "I never saw the big picture of what they were putting together to learn and discover. I had all the puzzle pieces, and I laid them out and arranged them by color. I didn't put the puzzle together, I just organized the pieces. What picture that painted, I don't even know.

"I played each clip and explained what it was," said Gary, noting that he talked about each shot and answered questions in front of the Senate for about half a day. "I was on the stage for a good four hours."

All of the footage was put on a private server and hardware-encrypted. Gary explained that hardware encryption is a step above typical software encryption, which involves a four- to ten-digit pass code. "Hardware-encrypted means it was encrypted on a chip that was in the machine. You don't have a physical key, and this is 128-bit encryption. It limited the physical machines this could be viewed on." This way, material could be sent over the Internet, but it couldn't be hacked because of the encryption key.

By the next week, another person had created a geospatial map, plotting where each clip had been shot from. "They could tell what corner each photographer was standing on, so they could match angles. Then they went through and cleaned up the footage that should go back out and be released to the public.

Many shots were sequestered," Gary said. The close-ups of people jumping out of windows and shots of them hitting the ground were withheld, along with those of the second plane going into the building and the wing ripping apart.

"Some of those shots were so awful, and that might be one reason they were sequestered, but the primary reason was that it showed weakness. They didn't want other people saying that was a great idea, and it was also forensic evidence," Gary said, adding that his gut feeling was that they didn't want people to see those same awful shots over and over again. "But when did that ever stop the media?"

Gary pointed out that there was no footage released of the plane hitting the Pentagon. "That plane hit in the area of the Pentagon that had just been refurbished," he said, adding that it been a three-year undertaking, and they were putting the finishing touches on it. "They had beautiful new meeting rooms and offices, and I was the resident expert in the systems they already had in place."

Gary believes that 9/11 was a turning point for our country for a couple of reasons. "It stripped away the naiveté of the military's manipulation of the media. It was never more apparent that the media has always been a tool for government to help control the population and the message going out to the people. It always has been, but never was it more apparent to this extent that they could motivate an entire country. We reacted just the way the government wanted us to act. The message was that the evil-doers, the Taliban, were bad people who like to blow things up. The government crafted that message, and we all drank the Kool-Aid."

The technology at the time of 9/11 was still shy of hitting today's easy access to video cameras. "That was the last time the government could have controlled such a huge message, because that would be impossible to do now," Gary pointed out, adding that the resulting media message was the last true example of programmed patriotism. "We were spoon-fed an image of what they wanted us to see, and they all asked us to feel a certain way about it. We felt a patriotic remorse about that, and the country was behind it. It defined us as 'the Americans,' fighting against 'the evil-doers'—the terrorist nations of the world—in the Axis of Evil."

In the days following the attacks, Gary felt that he was doing his share in the war against terrorism. "Like everyone else, I felt patriotic. I became more vigilant with what I thought were my parameters of personal safety, and that's how we were all meant to feel." The ability to run such interference now is impossible, and everyone can see the most unspeakable acts of terrorism, if they so desire.

"The message was that we were blind sided on 9/11, hit unaware," said Gary. "Were we provoking them? Or were we just sitting there quietly, minding our own business, and they just came and smacked us? The message was that we were sucker-punched, and now we have to stand up to them."

And yet one has only to remember the first World Trade Center bombing in 1992 to agree that the area was already targeted. But the reasons for such hatred and destructive acts are still unknown.

"In the weeks following 9/11, President Bush put forth more crafted messages, like 'We don't know why they do the things they do, that's what makes them terrorists. They just hate Americans. They hate the western way of life and were after all of us…' but that was not their message. I think it was anti-government, anti-CIA. They were angry with us for not supporting them after the Afghanistan war.

"It was the Cold War that led up to the Taliban making us the target. You don't get smacked in the back of the head for no reason. What did we do to deserve that animosity?"

July 3, 2002

RIDE "4" AMERICA

SINCE THEY LEFT OKLAHOMA CITY ON APRIL 24TH, 2002, four cowboys and their convoy of Buffalo Soldiers have been creating quite a spectacle along highways throughout the eastern half of America as they wagon-train across Missouri, Illinois, Indiana, Ohio, Pennsylvania, Maryland, the District of Columbia, New Jersey and New York all summer long.

Through drenching storms and muggy heat, their sojourn will be completed on September 11th in New York City, with the cowboys tipping their hats to the thousands who sacrificed their lives one year before in a terrorist act that surpassed even Oklahoma City.

"We want the victims of terrorism to know that we are willing to share in their grief and hardship. Our ride from the Alfred P. Murrah building in Oklahoma City to the site of the World Trade Center is just a token of the heartache and pain we feel for them. Our sacrifice is small by comparison, but we know that we can make a difference," said Tim Meyers, president of Oklahoma Western Heritage, Inc. The riders have established a non-profit organization and are collecting money to help the children orphaned by the tragedy.

A rider-less horse named Scout heads the troop, his saddle adorned with symbols of our fallen heroes: patches and badges and a fireman's boot hanging from the stirrup. The group trotted into Butler for a pre-scheduled meet-and-greet at the Butler Farm Show grounds on July 3rd, 2002.

These cowboys know about terrorism and lives shattered by an evil plot. Meyers said he considers the bombing of the Murrah Building in Oklahoma City a terrorist act, right along with the events of 9/11, which is represented by their use of the number "4" in Ride "4" America. Soon after watching the Twin Towers collapse on television, the spiritually-moved cowboy felt compelled to travel to the other three sites -- Shanksville, the Pentagon and Ground Zero -- to raise money for the children left orphaned by the tragedy and to show his support for the fighting spirit which runs through the veins of this country's western heritage.

"I got together with a good bunch of people, and we thought about how we were gonna get there, 'cause that's a long way off," recalled Meyers, "and I said, 'The only way we're gonna get there is on horseback!'" With that statement and three other cowboys: Robert Malone, Fred Bell and Gary Conger, Ride "4" America became a mission.

When VisionQuest National—a program which sponsors horseback journeys through the western United States for inner-city children—got wind of the cowboys' mission, they offered to escort the men with rotating groups of troopers and a wagon train.

According to wagon master Rich Valdez, the troopers consist of 26 children, ages 13 to 18, who represent the "Buffalo Soldiers." This is a Native American term that was used in the 1800s by Cheyenne warriors out of respect for the fighting ability of the 10th Cavalry. Later, all African-American soldiers eventually became known as Buffalo Soldiers.

The current crop of kids originated in Gettysburg, Pennsylvania, where they were trained in cavalry tactics. "We've got 30 to 35 horses on the road," said Valdez, "and we've been respected so far. Some people on the highway ignore us, but many give us their blessings. This is the experience of a lifetime for these kids."

Eighteen year old Mark (last name withheld for privacy reasons), who was pulled off of the mean streets of West Philadelphia by VisionQuest, is a shining example of an already successful journey. "I didn't know real cowboys even existed, but I've found that cowboys are open-minded people," he said, dressed smartly in his soldier outfit and as polite as a Boy Scout. "My life before this was cut-throat. I didn't care about being successful, and I did so much wrong. Now I'm trying to give back something -- I have so many regrets -- but now I have the opportunity to do good. Most likely, I'd be dead if it weren't for this."

Cowboy Gary Conger acknowledged the benefits of having the kids along as escorts. "We couldn't do it without them," he told the audience in Butler. As an emergency medical technician and firefighter captain, Conger was deeply affected by 9/11. "Cowboys are different," he said, "we have deep-seated souls, and we're doing this for the children who were orphaned, as well as for those who died."

Along their route, the cowboys have been accepting donations to keep the costs of the journey as low as possible. Michelle

Summerill and Mike Cultter of Mars EMS saw the horses and kids riding into Butler on Monday and decided to check out the situation. "We figured it was VisionQuest," said Cultter, "and when we found out what they were doing, we asked how we could help." For the first time in her life, Summerill found herself in the local Agway buying three days' worth of oats, hay and firewood, and Cultter borrowed his father's truck to haul it to the Butler Farm Show.

"I think what they're doing is amazing," said Summerill. "It's a strange donation for Mars EMS to buy things for horses, but it's definitely worth it."

Their next stop will be Shanksville, arriving by Sunday, July 14th, where they have a pot luck dinner planned with the local community. The evening will include an equestrian show by the troopers, as well as live music and storytelling. On the morning of July 15th, the cowboys will participate in a Flight 93 memorial ceremony, which will culminate in their placing the Oklahoma state flower at the crash site.

Sonny Malone, a cowboy and direct descendent of the Osage Indian tribe, said, "If anyone has any kind of heartfelt knowledge about what happened on 9/11, it's Oklahomans. Everything changed in that one instant. Now we've put aside our regular lives to do this, and we don't worry about the weather, the cold, the heat, and the ticks, because we're doing this to get those orphaned kids some money so that Bin Laden can't rob us of their potential. We're Americans, and united we stand."

September 11, 2002

9/11 MURAL: TERROR TRANSFORMED

GRACING THE STAIRWELL of Butler's Intermediate High School is a magnificent 16-foot-high, 4-foot-wide artistic collaboration by art students, representing peace, patriotism, and Americans coming together in the wake of disaster: Two towers, the Statue of Liberty superimposed on them from ground level, reach into the heavens as doves ascend out of the embrace of the flag.

"It made people feel a lot better because there was no terrorist aspect in it, it's symbolic, and it was nice to see the building intact," explained eleventh-grade art club student Stephanie Heitzer, 16, of Summit Township. "I did a lot with the doves, and the big dove in the center -- that was mine. The doves signify lost souls and a more happy feeling that people are free and going to a better place." Art teacher Erich Campbell's brainchild, the mural has helped teachers and students cope with an event that changed their lives -- for the better.

"So many people died, but September 11th has more meaning for the people who lived," said Heitzer. "Life has changed so much, and everything's in a different perspective now. [The events of Sept. 11] completely shocked me, I couldn't speak, and it changed my life completely. I think about things differently now, and I'm starting to realize what's really important -- family and friends -- and I've grown up a lot."

She's also discovered the impact of art in expressing her emotions. Heitzer said, "I'm thinking more about art now, after I realized that the more you feel about it, the better it is, and it was such an awesome feeling. Now I want to go to art school."

"This is the most striking example of [Erich Campbell's] impact on students," said John Wyllie, principal of Butler Intermediate. "What he draws out of students, and how he gets them to express themselves is simply phenomenal, and it came out across our entire student body. Our kids got very involved in contributing to the relief efforts, and this is something that is very important to them."

Two years ago, Campbell had collaborated with elementary school students from Shaler to create an enormous mural to memorialize the shootings at Columbine, regarding kids and violence in society, and how good things, like unity and love, can come out of violent situations. The 16-foot-wide by 6-foot-high mural went on exhibit at the Andy Warhol museum in May of 2000.

Campbell was thrilled with the success of his first mural, but didn't consider doing another similar project until last year. He had just gotten married in July of 2001, and he was itching to do another large-scale mural. "I wanted it to deal with something in society or culture," he said, "and our first club doesn't meet until the end of September."

In the first days of last September, Campbell was starting another school year with a project in mind for his monthly art club students. Then the unthinkable happened. "After September 11th, I knew I had to do something," he said. "What idea I had before that, I can't even remember."

As if driven by an unseen force, he began sketching his ideas onto paper before presenting them to the students in the club. "We talked a lot about design and what they felt after 9/11 -- how this changes everything -- and this mural needs to visually represent how we all came together, while still remembering the towers at the same time. America is coming out of it stronger than ever. I didn't want a mural with the towers on fire or anything showing death, in fact, the only thing red in the mural is the flag."

Campbell has been teaching in Butler County schools since 1995, after graduating from Bethany College in West Virginia as a graphic design/advertising major and getting his teaching certificate. His wife, Kristen Diulus Campbell, described the big, burly teacher as a strict disciplinarian who's completely devoted to fostering teamwork and talent in his students.

"He's a Mister Clean-type of guy, and he looks like a big muscle-head," said Kristen, adding that in addition to teaching art, her husband coaches football and track. "But Erich's really into artistic expression -- painting famous people, events and situations kids can learn from. Not many school districts have strong art programs, and Butler wasn't any different before Erich came. Now they need another teacher to take the overflow."

"I walk by it every day, and some days it brings a smile to your face and sometimes it gives you chills," said Campbell. "Nothing is certain anymore, and the flag wrapping around the towers is symbolizing America's pulling together and comforting those involved directly. The doves represent peace, lives lost, and the fact that we need to be at peace with ourselves and one another."

Campbell added a most poignant touch to the mural when he incorporated the Statue of Liberty into the project. Said Heitzer, "Mr. Campbell comes up with the best ideas. We all knew it needed something else, something to signify America more than just the flag and the towers, and the statue represents that."

Approximately 20-25 students had a hand in the creation, according to Calvin Lumley, of Butler Township, also in 11th grade. "I helped our teacher in every way I could," said the 16-year-old who spent every spare moment last year to work on the mural, especially focusing on the words that cover the buildings. "We wrote the Pledge of Allegiance and other words relating to freedom onto the sides of the buildings instead of windows," he said. "I felt it was special while I was working on it, but when it was completely done, it was amazing so see the high caliber of the work. I didn't think I had it in me."

What's most amazing to faculty and parents is that the mural has been placed in a high-traffic area of the school, yet the students have not done anything to deface it.

"The students have respect; they know not to disturb it in any way," said Lumley. "It makes me feel good that I could have a hand in something that was meant for 9/11. It symbolizes the remembrance for me, but it also feels like it happened yesterday."

"The mural never ceases to surprise me -- I'm in awe of it," said Heitzer. "It's so huge, that no matter where you stand -- on the platform in front of it, on the stairs below it, looking up at it -- it gives you a really good feeling."

Campbell and his students kept the project under wraps while they worked on the mural, which he estimates took about 35 hours to complete, but Principal Wyllie had a few opportunities to view the work in progress. "He had come to me with the idea for the project and I certainly encouraged him. I got some private viewings, and even near completion, laid flat across tables, it was impressive, but once it was mounted in the stairwell, it's absolutely inspiring," said Wyllie.

"For the first three weeks it was up, it was very common to be walking past it, and you'd have a few people just standing there looking at it. There would be some hushed comments, but people who've been in the building for many years just stopped and stared," he said. "I really wasn't concerned about the students defacing it, because they are so respectful due to the magnitude of the event and knowing that fellow students did that."

Campbell and his wife have been in contact with people who work at an office at Ground Zero, and they have expressed interest in exhibiting the mural in their lobby, but amidst everything else that is being sent to New York to commemorate the event, it isn't possible to send it there now.

"Maybe it could go there next September 11th," said Campbell, who's eager for the other people to see what he and his students have done. "I just want to get it out there for people to see, and maybe it could stay right here in Pittsburgh, in PPG Place or the USX Tower, or even at the stadiums."

"It's a piece that virtually every American can relate to," said Wyllie. "I know the students who produced it would be extremely proud to have additional people look at it, and I would support something like that, but when we put it up, we put it up permanently. The structure we built to support it was made with the idea that it would be there as long as the building was there. It was such a grand historical event that even 20 years from now it's not going to be irrelevant. A large part of me would be sad if it were to leave it's home permanently. It could go on tour, but it should eventually come back, because this is its home."

November 20, 2002

MURAL ON THE MOVE

THE STUDENTS AND FACULTY of Butler Intermediate High School knew that they were in possession of something very special, something they needed to share with the world.

"I'm amazed at how easy it was to get it out there," said art teacher Erich Campbell of the breathtaking, 16-foot high, 4-foot wide mural, which was created by the school's art students out of their empathy for the tragedy of the World Trade Center's collapse.

Since its creation -- just after the events of September 11, 2001, claimed the lives of thousands of office workers -- the towering portrayal of doves ascending from two buildings wrapped in the embrace of the flag has been Butler's secret treasure. Campbell, however, has been eager to let the secret out since 9/11's first anniversary. "The students will miss it, but they all understand that it's got to go somewhere; that other people need to see it," he said.

Campbell's mother-in-law, Patty Diulus-Myers of Mt. Lebanon, was the driving force behind the mural's debut in One PPG Plaza -- just in time for Light-up Night. As a partner at Jackson Lewis LLP, a nationwide labor and employment law firm which has an office in the PPG building, Diulus-Myers brought Butler Intermediate's mural to the attention of her colleagues in the company's New York office.

"Our office in New York was particularly impacted by the 9/11 tragedy because our employees watched the whole thing," she recalled. "People in NYC really appreciate that people outside of NYC were impacted by their tragedy. When we showed a picture of the mural to the managing partner of our firm, a New Yorker, he thought the mural should come to NYC. 'There's this wonderful treasure hidden in Butler, PA,' he said, 'this should be on display.'"

That idea was the start of what Campbell hopes will eventually become a tour. He decided that the tour should begin in Pittsburgh. Said his proud mother-in-law, "I called the PPG building management and said, 'Do you want to see something really spectacular?' PPG has some very unique displays, and I thought it would be very appropriate."

PPG property manager Susan Neidbale agreed. "I sent the photo up to our owner contact, and he liked it a lot and wanted to put it someplace where everyone could see it," she said. They had hoped to put the mural in the building for the 9/11 anniversary, but there wasn't enough time, so Neidbale targeted the Christmas season instead.

Since it is considered a permanent part of Butler Intermediate High School, Campbell had to get permission from the superintendent before taking the mural to Pittsburgh. "They let me take a van down, brought a substitute [teacher] in for me and let me take a teacher business day, which gave me the whole day to take it down. They were just unbelievable," said Erich of Butler's school administrators. "Everybody -- from maintenance to the principal to the superintendent -- have made it so easy for me to do this. I didn't have to go through any red tape."

The mural now hangs on the wall between a bank of elevators in the east lobby of One PPG Plaza and can be seen through the glass windows of the 50-ft. high vestibule, tucked a respectable distance away from the glitz and glitter of Christmas. "You just stand there and stare at it," said Neidbale. "The longer you look at it, you see something else. It's very moving."

"I drove down [last Friday] and got there around 9:30. It was a beautiful morning, and people were just going about their business, much like September 11th, 2001," recalled Campbell. "Driving to the city, I thought about the fact that nobody understands what's coming, but for me it was a moment that's come full-circle."

March 19, 2003

MAIL CALL

CAPT. JOE RILEY'S REQUEST WAS SIMPLE: "I have some single, young Marines that don't receive any mail," he wrote from a computer in a sand-blasted tent in the middle of the desert in Kuwait. "It would be great if [someone] would be willing to mail these young Marines a letter or a care package."

Drenched in sand, flea-bitten and stinking from the inability to bathe, the only bright spot in a soldier's day is receiving mail. "All the Marines greatly anticipate mail call," explained Riley in emails to his mother, Pat Riley, in Zelienople (PA).

Riley, 33, a career soldier now stationed out of Camp Lejeune, North Carolina, grew up in Zelienople and graduated from Seneca Valley High School in 1987. He is married and has a 20-month-old daughter. Although he himself is blessed with a slew of family and friends to make mail call an exciting part of each day, Riley decided to let his community know that 37 of the 163 Marines in his unit were often deprived of such a morale booster.

On February 18, Riley's mother helped him start a letter-writing campaign designed to lift the spirits of his neglected fellow Marines -- and the public's response has been overwhelming and far-reaching as a multitude of schools, organizations and businesses heed the call for mail.

"I sent four emails to our other four children, plus two more emails to [a local newspaper and school]," said Pat Riley, "and suddenly it's taken on a life of its own." She also gave her son's letter to Pam Hall, owner of the Super Style Beauty Shop in Harmony, and was shocked by the reaction of its patrons.

"The beauty shop has had people donate so much; we packed up 23 2'x 2' boxes and mailed them last Saturday morning. This is the second group of boxes, and there are still more to go," she said, marveling at the kindness and generosity of strangers. "People have given money to pay for the postage, and they've donated everything under the sun. It seems they all wanted to do something to show their appreciation, but no one knew what to do."

In his correspondence, Riley specifically asked that teachers have their classes put together an effort to brighten the soldiers' days. The email was forwarded to Seneca Valley Public Relations Director Linda Andreassi, who immediately notified district principals and teachers of Riley's request and got an overwhelming response. This gave birth to Seneca Valley's "Project Enduring Freedom."

Riley compiled a list of the names and addresses of the 37 Marines, along with a description of their plight, for the students. "Mail is a big pick-me-up for the Marines," he wrote. "My Marines work 18 hours a day, every day, without a break, and remain motivated to serve our country. Even just a letter telling them that they are doing a good job and are appreciated would be great."

He also provided a list of items that would help get his soldiers through their ordeal. "Things any young Marine would need are newspapers, snacks, beef jerky, Tylenol for headaches, candy, Band-Aids, foot powder, baby wipes (in lieu of showers), sports magazines, AA batteries, etc... We are broken off from the outside world, so any newspapers or current events magazines would be great," he added.

According to 7th grade English teacher Leslie Russell, her students were visibly affected. "When I read the original letter from Captain Riley to my students two weeks ago, I could see their reactions as they considered being far away from home with no one to write or show that they are cared about," said Russell. She read each additional communication from Riley and showed the children photos he emailed of the Marines' surroundings in Kuwait, complete with camels.

"I reminded them that this land was once ancient Mesopotamia, which they had been studying in Ancient Civilizations class with their Social Studies teacher," Russell explained. "I think that made a big impression on them as well, but I think what hit them the hardest was hearing that the Marines got no hot showers and no fast food!"

On March 14, approximately 125 7th grade students (the project is district-wide) gathered all the items they'd collected for the soldiers in the cafeteria of the seventh- and eighth-grade middle school, located in Harmony, and put together 37 shoe-box care packages for the Marines, plus a special one for Riley. The week before, they each sent a letter to one of the soldiers on the list, expressing their appreciation for being on the front lines.

At the tender ages of 12 and 13, the youngsters were thrilled to be helping people they perceived as their protectors. "This is big," said Vicki Crawford, 12, of Cranberry. "This project means a lot to me, because I feel like I'm really helping them, and they're protecting our country."

"Everyone should do this," said 13-year-old Justin Skowronski, also of Cranberry. "We should all show support for the Marines and their families."

Both 7th graders talked about their fears and the way their lives have been changed by terrorism. "Before Sept. 11th, I didn't know what terrorism was," admitted Crawford. "Now I know that it's people who want to harm us for no reason, just because they don't like us -- that's like judging a book by its cover."

"My hope," said Russell, "is that [this will prompt] other communities to 'adopt' one of their hometown men or women and implement the same sort of project we're doing in the Seneca Valley School District. Aside from our personal beliefs about the necessity for war, the military personnel deserve whatever support we can muster for them."

Support for Riley's Marines has finally begun to show up in the military police battalion's mail bags, and he reported that the soldiers are ecstatic. "I'm not sure how you got the word out to the eastern half of the U.S., but thank you so much," Riley told his mom in a recent email. "Sounds like these Marines can expect much mail in the future. It means more to them than you can imagine."

April 9, 2003

HOPE ACROSS AMERICA

ON SEPTEMBER 17, 2001, Haine Elementary School principal Dr. Melvin Steals received a written request from then fifth-grader Michael Gorrio that made him weep with emotion.

"I would like to do something for the kids who lost their moms and dads on Sept. 11th," wrote Michael Gorrio, who was 10 years old at the time. "I would like to start a collection at Haine School for their college education. I would like to ask the kids to bring in their nickels, dimes and quarters to raise $1,000. After we raise $1000, I would like to invite every grade school, middle school and high school in Pittsburgh, the state of Pennsylvania and America to do the same. I'm writing to request your support with the collection so the boys and girls who lost their moms and dads on Sept. 11 will have their college education paid for."

The wounds from what happened on September 11th were still very fresh, and Steals had been personally affected by the tragedy. "My son had a college classmate in one of the [World Trade Center] buildings, and one of our students' grandmother and aunt were on that airplane," he recalled.

Steals immediately went to his superiors in the Seneca Valley school district to see what they could do about Michael's request and encountered the first hurdle. "There was a lot of interest, but the school district didn't want to handle the money," said Steals. So he turned around and approached Reverend Larry Homitsky of the United Methodist Church in Cranberry. "The church was willing to collect the money and hold it for us until we were ready to move it," said Steals. "It seemed like a divine purpose, like Michael was part of a bigger design that I couldn't see."

Michael and his father, Carlos Gorrio, a sales rep for Pfizer Pharmaceuticals, coined the slogan, "Hope Across America -- Young People Making A Difference," and pasted the phrase on approximately 300 plastic jars that were donated by a pretzel company. Michael and his friends placed the jars in every classroom at Haine and Rowan schools, as well as Pine-Richland Elementary School.

And he didn't stop there. "Another place we raised money was Oxford Athletic Club," said Michael. His mother, Laurie, teaches aerobics at the Oxford Club, and with her bosses' blessing, the Gorrio family sold T-shirts sporting the Hope Across America logo and flag pins they made out of beads. That event alone raised over $1000.

After 18 months, Michael had collected just over $5,000, which was recently deposited into a college fund for 16-year-old Andrew and 9-year-old Matthew Picarro, who lost their father, Ludwig Picarro, in the 9/11 disaster.

Michael hopes that his success in fundraising for a worthy cause will inspire others to follow suit. "It shows that anyone, even kids, can stand up, help out and contribute to make a difference in the world."

July 1, 2003

BOYS TO MEN

JANICE DEHART SEARCHED FOR HER BOY among the throng of soldiers returning from a recent tour of duty overseas. She'd been waiting for this moment for two long years. Where was he?

Then her eyes settled on a smile. It was Mark. But this wasn't the boy to whom she'd said good-bye two years earlier. It was a man she was meeting for the first time.

"It was an emotional day, and I didn't recognize my son because he filled out so much," she laughed. "He was a skinny little thing when he left, and it was only after he smiled that I knew who he was."

Once school boys looking for a way to help pay for their upcoming college tuition, Mark DeHart and Scott Garing entered the Army National Guard during a time of peace. In one horrible moment, just months after they had graduated from Seneca Valley high school, the two became active soldiers instead of students, forced to leave their families to set out on an unknown journey.

The changes -- internal and external -- that have occurred in their sons have been glaringly apparent to the mothers who feel deprived of witnessing their magical transformation from boys to men.

"As much as I hate to say it, I do think the Army's been good for him," said Scott's mother, Debbie Garing. "It's opened his eyes and broadened his horizons. Now he's interested in the government. I still see the kid in him, but there's been a lot of maturity."

She said that, since returning home, Scott has opted to take some time off to get back into the swing of things, but he's still volunteering as an emergency medical technician alongside his father, Scott Garing, Sr., an Allegheny General Hospital flight nurse.

Home since early February, "Scott's life has been Army for two years, and he wants to enjoy some freedom before he finally gets to start college," said Debbie Garing, as she alluded to a looming possibility. "Then again, he may get booted back over there."

Stationed in Germany, Garing and DeHart were spared from fighting the war in the Middle East. And their mothers slept more easily at night, knowing that their sons weren't battling deplorable, dangerous conditions in the desert -- yet it's taken time for them to get used to the fact that their children have been forever changed by the experience.

"I was on my own [in the Army], and I learned that there is a lot more to life than just living here," said Garing, a native of Harmony. "Going overseas gives you a different perspective that most people don't get. I thought I'd live at home and go to college and stay here for the rest of my life, but I've learned that everything's got a twist to it."

Off-duty, DeHart wandered around the southern German village of Honefels, taking in the experience of living in another culture, but he found it impossible to escape the sharp pangs of homesickness for the tight-knit family and girlfriend he had left behind in Franklin Township.

"We could take leave to travel, but I didn't go far. I just looked around," he said. "I missed knowing the speed limit and the language; I missed Burger King, Arby's and Wendy's, and I missed being on the same time schedule, because calling home was difficult. It was rough to be up that late to talk to them."

Well aware of how difficult life is for the soldiers stationed in the desert, both Garing and DeHart nevertheless wished they could have done more.

Not that their task in Germany wasn't inherently dangerous -- their mothers emphasized that it definitely was -- and danger still may lurk in the distance.

"Part of their job was to look for bombs," said Debbie Garing, "and Scott had volunteered for that duty! There were three check-points on the gate, and their job was to check the cars. Scott was at the first check." She explained that the 128th Forward Support Battalion, Company A, of Butler, is normally a supply unit, but the soldiers had to be re-trained to function like military police on base.

DeHart's mom continues to live with the fear that the Army will call her boy back at any moment, further delaying his college education... or worse. "He could have had a year in school if it hadn't been for the war. Now he's been out of school for two years, but he chose to do the service, and when Sept. 11th happened, there was nothing anyone could do," she said. "We all had to take it in stride, knowing he was going to leave."

Even though Janice DeHart knows that her son's situation could have been much worse, and she's grateful to have him home, she's still waiting for the proverbial "other boot" to drop. "I have the biggest fear that when it comes time for him to start college, they'll be re-deployed out. I'm very afraid of that, and I hope my gut's wrong, but I don't know if I could handle him being gone again," she said.

Following in his father's footsteps, Garing plans to attend Butler County Community College in the fall and study nursing, as well as working as an EMT for an ambulance company.

DeHart will attend Slippery Rock in the fall to study special education. And in approximately one year, he plans to wed his high school sweetheart, Maria Mullet.

"Marks's going to be 21 tomorrow, and it's hard to accept," his mother admitted. "When he came back home, he was a young man. It's hard to let those apron strings go. I didn't get to see him mature into that young adult; he did that over there. I thought at first that I got my teenage son back, and I learned real quick that he's been doing things by himself for the last eight months and can now do things on his own. He's still here, but he's gone on to adulthood. I had to pace myself and readjust to him, and I did. It hurt, but I accept it."

Mark is the third of four children in the DeHart family, and his mother is now shifting her focus to teenage son Arthur, the last DeHart to leave the nest. "At least I still have one more to go," she added.

Both moms have also noticed quite a positive change in the way their sons now relate to their families.

"When the family wasn't there, that made him sit and think what family is all about," said Janice DeHart. "He would call his grandmother and talk to her once a week to make sure she was okay, because even though he knew she was fine, he still had to hear her voice. Now that he's home, he's calling and telling her anytime something goes on. He does more with his nephew, Tyler. Passing the football, watching TV with him, and he's also closer to his nieces now than when he left."

Debbie Garing said she also sees her son showing much more of an interest in his family. "He makes a point of seeing his grandparents, and he's acting on a more mature level. He keeps his finances in order and pays his bills on time, which, for a 20 year old, is pretty good. He's responsible."

"It's weird to be a foreigner," remarked Garing, who got along well with the German people he came in contact with. "It's completely different, and teaches you a valuable lesson not to make fun of foreigners here, but to try to help them out. Some Germans were real nice to us, and we'd joke around with them, and some were [nasty] when we had to check their cars, but we were just doing our jobs."

"It was an awesome trip I went on," said DeHart, "but there's definitely no place like home."

July 1, 2003

DISCIPLINE: A RITE OF PASSAGE

DRIVING THEIR 16-YEAR-OLD SON, ANDY, to Fork Union Military Academy (FUMA) in Central Virginia three years ago was a heart-wrenching experience for Michael and Tammy Hodak. "Taking him 300 miles from home and leaving him with a bunch of men from the South was hard for his mother and his sister, but I knew he could handle it," says Hodak. "It was difficult for me too, but I wasn't thinking about me. I was thinking about what was best for him."

We all want the best for our children, but in our desire to make them happy, we sometimes lose sight of what they really need -- consistent discipline and adult supervision.

According to the American Academy of Pediatrics (AAP), "The word discipline refers to the system of teaching and nurturing that prepares children to achieve competence, self-control, self-direction, and caring for others." It's not about punishment; it's about teaching kids how to become successful adults.

"As much as kids tell us they don't want boundaries and limits, deep down inside, kids really do want them," says Peter's Township High School guidance counselor Shelly Saba. "They innately know that that's how their parents show them that they care."

And that's not to say that parents don't care, but as a generation, we're certainly not the disciplinarians our parents were.

A STRICT ALTERNATIVE

Removing a child from his family and friends and sending him away to a military academy may sound like a harsh sentence, but for Andy -- now 19 and studying liberal arts at Columbus State University in Columbus, Ohio -- it was the key to unlocking his potential.

According to Robert Grant, FUMA's director of guidance, "Because of the way our society is structured, there's not enough structure and stability in households. Most of our students are good guys, but they got lost in a big school and maybe needed more attention than they received. A lot had a false start to high school because of too many distractions."

At FUMA, distractions like video games, CDs, cell phones, cars and stereo systems are removed, and upper school students focus on one class at a time, which lets them concentrate their class and study time on a single area of content.

Grant says that signs that a child needs more guidance than what's offered in a typical public or private day school can begin to emerge in middle school. "If [a child] has typically done well at school and had good test scores and then their grades start slipping, that's a red flag. If they're focusing their time and attention on less active pursuits like video games, or they're spending too much time with friends who think that school achievement is not important, that's another.

"And if you sense a change in their values that's dramatically different from the way that they're raised, that's a warning sign, too."

Andy's first two years at Peters Township High School had been unproductive. Lacking self-confidence, skipping classes and sassing his parents, Andy's grades had slipped to unacceptable depths. His parents knew he had potential, but they felt that they were unable to control his behavior.

And then a neighbor told them about FUMA, and Andy was enrolled in his junior year.

"We noticed the change in six weeks," recalled Hodak, noting that when Andy arrived home for the first time, his own mother didn't even recognize him. "When he got off the airplane, he was in uniform, and his mom thought he was a soldier coming home from Iraq. She was looking for her little boy she left in Fork Union, and a 6-foot-tall soldier came back in his place."

That Christmas, Andy made the Dean's List. And as he began excelling at Fork Union, his confidence soared, which brought about more achievements. "According to the brass at the academy, Andy was a born leader," said Hodak, noting that his son was the first student in FUMA's history to be selected to attend officer training in his first year. He subsequently trained at Ft. Lee with the 101st Airborne Rangers and now walks with pride and confidence as he contemplates a bright future.

"If you think you have the ability to compete with their TV, radio and the friends at school, you may have their attention for six to eight minutes a day," says Hodak. "I don't have the educational background to teach a child what he needs to learn about in school. I'm a contractor and I can't home school, but I knew that at Fork Union, they could do what I couldn't."

"We don't want our kids to be uncomfortable and upset, but in real life it's not that way," says Grant, noting that FUMA has parents sign a statement of support. "They must agree to stand behind us when the student needs it. There are punishments built in, and there's no way to get out of it.

"All parents talk about how important education is, but we enforce it. That's your main responsibility, and that's why we take away all the fun things. Fun things aren't bad, but your education is the most important thing, and if these are getting in the way, they have to go. Many kids have never experienced this before because no one has made them do anything."

THE MILITARY -- A PLACE OF STRUCTURE AND DISCIPLINE

Considering that they witnessed the most horrific act of terrorism this country has ever seen, teens today are especially stressed by world events. Now a war rages on -- and it's a war that some of our boys will actually fight.

Nathan Klock is a senior at Peters Township High School who wants to do his part in making the world a safer place, so he's joining the Navy as soon as he graduates in June. "I initially wanted to join the Marines," he says, "but my parents weren't supportive of that because they have a higher rate of death."

For some teens, the idea of joining the military is akin to salvation. After suffering from a troubled childhood and poor performance in school, Nathan has decided that the training he will receive in the military will enable him to do something productive that will help his country and turn his life around. "I need discipline," he says.

When asked why some teens do drugs, Nathan gave several reasons: "It's an antidote to boredom for a lot of kids, some kids do it to sabotage themselves, and some actually want to be sent away. Kids use drugs for all different reasons."

Nathan points to the breakdown of the traditional family model as the reason some kids run amuck. "Every child wants to spend time with their parents," he states. "We want you to come to our games and play basketball in the driveway with us. We want family dinners, and we want to play games and go jogging or fishing with you. We wish you didn't work so much, and we want you to tell us what to do. Don't be afraid to crack down and discipline us, because parents have to help their kids."

Petty Officer First Class James Betz is Washington County's naval recruiter. "People come in with a wide variety of reasons to join the Navy," he says. "Some join for benefits, some for guidance, some for travel opportunities, and many who just want to defend their country. I get a lot of people who come in and say, 'My life is going nowhere fast, and this could be a great option for me.'"

Patty Fisher of Canonsburg is a single mom who wishes her 20-year-old son, Jason, had joined the Navy, but he joined the Marine Corps instead. After graduating from boot camp last March, he went to Iraq in December.

"I think he felt the need to be part of the best, and he feels that Marines are the best trained, and it shows when they're over there (in Iraq)," says Fisher. "When I first saw him after boot camp, he had lost 20 pounds, and he was thin to begin with, but he was muscled and lean. Before he went in, he had bad posture and wore his pants baggy. Now he's straight as an arrow."

Thinking about her son, Fisher feels a mixture of pride and fear. "I have every faith he's going to be fine, and I pray a lot, for all of them," she says, acknowledging that the Marines were responsible for turning her young boy into a man. "They did what I couldn't do."

Fisher says that since he was five, Jason had to travel between his mother's home in Canonsburg and his father's home in Michigan, and he lacked self-confidence.

"I don't think a parent can give them that sense of confidence; that has to come from his peers and living on the edge. The training they go through also builds confidence and character," she points out, adding, "And whenever he comes home for a visit, the house is in perfect condition when he leaves."

Paul Abernathy is a U.S. Army reservist from South Fayette Township who served in Iraq during the start of the war. Now he's studying at the University of Pittsburgh for his masters in International Affairs. "I think a lot of people end up in the military because it offers a sense of direction, gives them a purpose, and the discipline gives them personal responsibility," Abernathy observes.

"Everyone wants to serve their country, but many are there because the military provides something that all the other organizations can't offer -- it allows them to see who they really are and the nature of their character."

TOO MUCH INFORMATION, TOO LITTLE COMMUNICATION

In this Information Age, it's become nearly impossible for today's parents to shelter their children from the fact that there is evil in the world. Thanks to television and the Internet, childhood is no longer a time of blissful unawareness.

Yet, at the same time, Saba says there's a serious lack of communication that needs to be addressed. "In the past, there was more of a sense of community, and parents naturally took care of other kids in the neighborhood," Saba points out. "If another parent six doors away saw a kid doing something wrong, they'd call his parents. Now they're afraid to do that.

"Parents need to talk to other parents," she adds. "Technology has brought us some great things, but it has limited face-to-face time and calling on the phone time. We need to get that sense of community back and know that someone is watching out for our kids."

Likewise, parents need to stay informed about their teens' performance at school, which Saba says is easy, thanks to Peters Township High School's Edline. This is a website where parents can log on daily and check student attendance, discipline, homework assignments and grades, which are updated regularly. But she adds that Edline should be used in conjunction with going to school, attending school performances and meeting with teachers face-to-face.

Saba acknowledges that it's often difficult to get teens to talk, but showing an interest in your child's life at school and asking questions is the best way to be informed.

"Ask kids each night if they have homework," she advises. "We do what we can on our end, but it helps to have cooperation from the parents as well, and it has to be a two-way street. And if a child says they don't have homework for two weeks in a row, you should be suspicious."

Unfortunately, there is now a greater danger to teens than

flunking out of school: highly addictive drugs.

One line of defense at the high school is the Peters Township Student Assistance and Referral Team, known as STAR Team, in which referrals about a student are made when warning signs, like sleeping in class or marks on the arm, are noticed. "Anyone can make a referral," says Saba, explaining that each referral is investigated. "If there's a referral made on a student, we send our information sheets to get feedback from the teachers, and then we meet as a team and we decide what to do. We get STAR referrals all the time."

Intervention specialist Jay Thornton then calls students' homes and alerts the parents before presenting them with the evidence.

When asked why teens still do drugs despite efforts to educate them on the dangers, Saba says, "With the developmental stage teens are in, they feel indestructible and don't think anything bad could happen to them. Sometimes it's a cry for help to get attention, but the more they hear [about the dangers of drugs] from different sources and people, the better."

Saba points out that setting boundaries and limits is also a way for parents to know if their kids are getting into trouble. "If they're doing drugs, these problems will be much more apparent," she says, "because the ones who are getting into at-risk behavior will not be following the rules."

July 11, 2003

FIGHTING TOGETHER

SCOTT GARING AND MARK DEHART were supposed to start college last fall. Instead, they're preparing to help fight the War on Terrorism.

Formerly active in his high school's ROTC program and interested in the tuition benefits, DeHart, 20, was the driving force behind getting his buddy Scott to join the Butler Army National Guard after they graduated from Seneca Valley High School in 2001. This was just months before the events of September 11th would cause the 128th Forward Support Battalion, Company A of Butler, to be immediately deployed to an undisclosed location overseas.

Garing was also planning to take advantage of the free tuition, but awaiting further instructions from the chain of command and getting through the holidays far from the family he loves, the 19-year-old Private First Class stated via email, "This is the only place I would rather be than at home. I am doing what makes my hometown proud: serving my country. Besides, this is why I joined the National Guard -- not for college tuition or benefits -- I joined to help out in times of need."

DeHart, now classified as SPC, which means specialist, made it clear that he has no regrets about joining the National Guard. "I joined the service for the career opportunity and to serve my country with honor," he said in an e-mail message, adding, "Yes, it is hard being away from my family over the holidays, but it is a learning experience for me."

In fact, most impressive to both families is the way their sons have grown and matured over the past two years. "When they left us, they were just young men, still very much teenagers, and now they're ready to take on the world," said DeHart's mother, Janice, in amazement. "They now think things through, and they make mature decisions."

Garing hadn't participated in high school ROTC like his friends, but when the idea came up, he embraced the opportunity. "We made him think hard about his decision," his mother, Deborah Garing, recalled. "He wanted to go [into the National Guard] when he was 17, and we had to sign the consent papers. We made him sit down and really think about it. We even had the recruiter here five times, but he wanted to do it, and you can't fault him; he didn't want to come out of school and be in debt.

"We kept asking Scottie, 'What would happen if...?' and here it is; if," said his mother. "He said that if he hadn't been in the National Guard, he definitely would have signed up after 9/11."

During those dark days in September 2001, the guys were busy getting their first taste of the army life. "The two of them never thought about being deployed or anything," recalled Janice DeHart. "They were still in AIT [training], where they went to learn about what they would do in the service."

Realizing that her son would feel the repercussions of what happened, Janice DeHart, a teacher's aide at Connoquenessing Valley Elementary, was devastated. "I kept getting phone calls about Mark, but he didn't even know what had happened, because the military didn't tell them anything," she said. "They had just finished up with basic training and schooling, came home and had time in between that, and then they got deployed. They didn't even know where they were going up until the last minute."

"I'm sorry Mark's gone, because he made the choice [to join the National Guard] before [September 11th] happened," said Mark DeHart, Sr., 42, a truck driver.

The elder DeHart, however, takes solace in the way soldiers are treated today. "The military is so well-equipped, and they do more to protect our soldiers that they don't seem to be expendable, like they did during the Viet Nam War with all the casualty reports," he said. "It was a different time and situation then, and during the Gulf War, our men and women in the service seemed to be more important than anything else. They take better care of them now, and it gives us a little bit of comfort -- but we want him back."

"A mom couldn't be prouder," said Janice DeHart. "Mark knows that the money they offered him for college will be there when he gets back. He doesn't feel betrayed or anything like that; he's honored to be doing something for the country." Both young men have left close-knit homes in Franklin Township, and DeHart's fiancée, Maria Mullett, 19, has been pining for her future husband since he left for basic training two years ago. "The hardest thing of all," said Mullett, "is that you don't realize what someone means to you until they are not here to share the special occasions." The couple plans to wed on Valentine's Day, 2004, and DeHart aspires to become a school teacher.

Garing and DeHart have missed many special family moments, especially the joy of spending time with their young nephews and nieces. "Mark's step-brother, David Galat, just had a baby; their first, and Mark missed that," said Janice DeHart. DeHart has two brothers; Arthur DeHart, 18, and David Galat, 30, of Elwood City, a sister; Jennifer Galat, 28, of Cranberry Township, three young nieces under two, and a nephew, 9. (The Galats are his half-siblings.)

Garing, on the other hand, is missing the toddler years of his only nephew, two-year-old Brandon Brubach, who's the son of his married older sister, Melanie Brubach, 27. "When Scottie calls, we mostly talk about my son and the things he's doing, because he feels he's missing out," said Brubach. "Our conversations are all about Brandon. When Scottie was home for a while, the two of them did a lot of things together. He wrote me an e-mail that he's disappointed he won't see Brandon open his gifts because he thinks it will be more fun this year."

Noted Brubach, "Scottie's grown up a lot in the last year and a half. He's a young man now instead of my teenage brother, and even though he's younger than I am, he's someone I can look up to." Garing also has a twin sister, Erin, and an older sister, Nicole, 21.

Long before joining the National Guard, Garing was already a hero-in-training. Emulating his father, Scott Garing, Sr., an emergency medical technician (EMT) and helicopter flight nurse for Allegheny General Hospital, the younger Garing started out as a junior firefighter at age 16. During his junior year of high school, he became an EMT, and in October, he and his father received an award for saving the life of a car accident victim who landed in the family's driveway last March. According to his parents, nursing is a career path Garing chose years ago. In the army, his rank is now Private First Class.

"It's scary, because I sit here and just wait," said Deborah Garing. "We have no control over what happens; other people do. He's our son, but Uncle Sam owns him now."

Their unit had a furlough during Christmas last year, marking this [2002] as the first year DeHart and Garing spent the holidays away from home. Refusing to let their son miss the holiday experience altogether, the DeHart family has decided to keep their Christmas tree up until he comes home. Said Janice DeHart, "We all decided that there are certain gifts between the family that will wait until he gets home."

In a tribute to their son, the Garings have their flag displayed outside and a candle burning in a window 24 hours a day. In addition, pictures of both Garing men in uniform (Garing Senior served in the Marines in the 1980's) hang on a wall.

"He's with us all the time in different ways," said Garing's mom. "On clear evenings, we say goodnight to the stars, knowing that wherever he is, he can see them too, even though the time is different. Silly things like that get us through."

Another means of support for the families of soldiers, called the Family Readiness Group (FRG), exists for each unit. Deborah Garing is vice-president of the Butler unit's FRG. "It's wives or husbands, mothers and dads who get together and discuss things," she explained. "We also have a calling tree to ask if anyone needs anything, even if it's just someone to talk to, and every year we organize a Christmas party and try to keep everyone (soldiers and families) in contact with one another."

Garing acknowledged that the stress of losing a breadwinner is harder on the families of married soldiers. "It's a hard adjustment for a wife to make," she said. "You hear a lot of stories, but the group has helped because I've gotten to know there's other mothers, fathers, husbands and wives who feel the same way I do, and we all look out for each other."

FIGHTING ALONE

Now single-handedly raising her son, Jared, who will turn two next week, 25-year-old Stacy Snyder can attest to the hardships of losing her husband, Wendale, to the threat of war.

"His contract [with the National Guard] was for six years, but they deployed him a few months before his contract was up and automatically re-enlisted him for another year," said Snyder. "He was home on September 11 [2001], but he didn't talk about it much. I was hoping he would never leave, but I knew it was a good possibility."

Snyder said her husband got his orders to leave shortly after 9/11 and was given a month and a half to get his affairs in order. Wendale "Bud" Snyder, 27, worked at the James Austin Company in Mars as a laborer, making bleach and cleaning products, and they're holding his job until he comes home.
"Bud worked nights and I worked days, and he and Jared spent their days together," said Snyder, who was formerly employed by Three Rivers Ice Cream company in Evans City. "I couldn't put Jared in daycare with his dad leaving, so I offered to work part time around my mom's schedule so she could watch my son, but then my employer decided there weren't any part time positions available, so I lost my job."

Unwilling to add to the stress of losing his father, Snyder

prefers to stay at home with their son and exist on unemployment and army benefits until her husband returns. "He was with my son all day, then all of the sudden he was gone," said Snyder from her son's point of view. "The first two months were the hardest [for Jared] because he was lost. He cried a lot and was very confused."

Bud Snyder hasn't been home for nearly a year now and doesn't expect to see his family until he can come back for good. "We want to see each other, but we don't want to confuse our son," Stacy Snyder explained. "We didn't go visit him overseas for the same reason."

She lamented, "When Jared's upset, he wants Daddy. Every time the phone rings, it's 'Daddy, Daddy'. Bud's been gone since he was 15 months old. There are so many changes when they're little; he misses so much in even one day." Snyder said her husband made a video for Jared before he left, which the child watches incessantly. The rest of the time, he's pretending to talk to his father on the phone and loves to color and draw and "send it to Daddy."

Signs of Christmas in the Snyder household in Jackson Township are almost non-existent. "I didn't put a Christmas tree up," she said. "Santa went to Grandma's house. I just have my cards up. My mother (Trudy Spurk of Evans City) has a tree and lights outside. I love Christmas, but this year I'm keeping it low-key."

She said they prefer to celebrate when her husband comes home. "I sent him some cookies and had done a scrapbook with a lot of pictures of my son, but he didn't want a bunch of things sent that he'd have to bring back."

The holidays are just a slice of the major events Bud Snyder will be absent for. "Bud's birthday is January 3rd, and my son's is the 11th, and he'll be gone for both. For now, we just have phone calls and letters."

Snyder's hoping her husband will get back in time to celebrate their second wedding anniversary in May. "We were high school sweethearts," she recalled. "We had plans to get married after high school, and we called it off and waited a couple of years. We planned to have a baby right away, but when we were married in Myrtle Beach, I didn't know I was already pregnant."

Looking back, Snyder is surprised at the twisted path her life has taken. "If I had known two years ago I'd be a single mom, I would have waited," she said, adding, "Then again, my son keeps me so busy, it makes it a lot easier. I guess it would be worse if I had to be alone."

October 18, 2004

PANEL DISCUSSION OF THE PATRIOT ACT

IN AN EFFORT TO EDUCATE THE PUBLIC about civil liberties issues, the National Council of Jewish Women (NCJW) hosted a panel discussion at Temple Ohav Shalom last Thursday, (10/14), regarding the facts and ramifications of the USA PATRIOT ACT to a mixed community crowd of nearly 100. Moderated by Jon Delano, KDKA Money and Politics Editor, five panelists examined the pros and cons of the PATRIOT ACT, and how it affects national security, as well as citizens' rights to privacy.

According to U.S. Attorney Mary Beth Buchanan, the PATRIOT ACT, which was almost unanimously passed by Congress 45 days after 9/11, is misunderstood by most Americans.

"The PATRIOT ACT is a series of laws that improve our [country's] ability to detect illegal immigrants; updates the law to be current with technology; and lets FBI agents share information with national security officials," said Buchanan, adding, "...and some people believe it limits our rights."

Vic Walczak, ACLU PA litigation director and Greater Pittsburgh Chapter legal director, said he agrees with 95 percent of the act, but criticized the secretive way in which investigations are being handled.

Walczak pointed out that Section 215 of the PATRIOT ACT gives the FBI the power to covertly spy on American citizens and permanent residents without probable cause, and a gag order prevents anyone from ever finding out about it. The ACLU is currently challenging this provision in court.

Cindy Richey, director of the Mt. Lebanon Public Library agreed with the ACLU's concerns. "Every citizen deserves equal access to information, as well as respect for their privacy, and library materials are confidential." She said that the Act puts those rights in jeopardy.

"If a librarian gets a subpoena, she can't tell anyone about it, not even a lawyer," said Walczak, noting that the gag order prevents citizens from knowing whether or not the government's authority is being used... or abused. "Who's going to be bold enough to stand up for somebody else's rights?" he questioned.

Pittsburgh FBI agent Jeff Killeen, however, made it clear that the Act is a necessary tool in protecting national security.

"On 9/11, I was standing in Somerset next to a hole in the ground, and I don't want to go there again," said Killeen. "This isn't history, this is now -- and the threat remains, because Al Qaida wants to hit us. Preventing another attack is our first priority."

Killeen noted that the FBI is aware of terrorist cells that currently exist in states including Oregon, Virginia, New York and Ohio. "The PATRIOT ACT has been very beneficial, because it allows [federal agencies] to share information," he said, adding that the FBI rarely resorts to section 215 measures.

Ken Gormley, professor of law at Duquesne University, talked about the historical aspect of executive branch power during times of crisis and war. "We are dealing with a shifting paradigm," he said, noting that with the events of 9/11, American soil has become a field of battle. "Some of these [legal] actions will most likely be deemed seditious."

Gary Schermer of McCandless is a teacher and an attorney, as well as a member of Temple Ohav Shalom. "I found the discussion fascinating," said Schemer afterwards. "I think the government has really gone too far [with the PATRIOT ACT], and there's a grave danger in not reigning them in.

"I'm interested in protecting our security, but giving [the government] carte blanche to make up the rules as you go is dangerous," he added. "Who would be the next target?"

Attorney George Kontos of Squirrel Hill said he was impressed by the information presented by the panelists. "The secrecy of the act was the most compelling part of the discussion," he said.

"Not being able to seek counsel seems contrary to a bedrock principal of our country. Initially, I thought certain portions [of the PATRIOT ACT] were important [to national security], but I continue to have reservations about the provisions discussed here."

In addition to discussing the PATRIOT ACT at Temple Ohav Shalom, the NCJW assembled other panelists to speak about reproductive rights at the South Hills JCC and O'Hara Elementary School in Fox Chapel in the month of October.

March 11, 2005

WAR STORIES

EVERY GENERATION HAS ITS OWN MEMORIES OF WAR, and not much has changed for infantrymen, observed Chief Warrant Officer Paul Sherry. When Sherry, 32, of Punxsutawney, spoke to the Shaler Rotary last Wednesday, he showed them images of wars, past and present. Several members of the rotary are WWII and Viet Nam veterans, who nodded with recognition as Sherry spoke of tracers in the sky and the thunderous boom of mortar fire.

As an air mission commander in charge of multiple aircraft, Sherry pilots a Black Hawk helicopter in the 1st Infantry Division of the Army on a variety of assignments. "But I'm still a soldier," he told the group. "We're still doing the same things [soldiers in previous wars have done]; we're still making a difference in people's lives."

Sherry returned to the states over a month ago after spending nearly a year in Iraq. But his parents, Anne and Mark Pennsy

-- along with everyone they know in Shaler Township and their former home in Punxsutawney -- were already privy to the details of their son's life on the front lines through Paul's monthly newsletter, *One Nighthawk*.

"People don't realize that there is so much good going on [in Iraq]," said Sherry. "It's a war, but we're there to help people. We allow people to sleep at night and know they'll wake up again in the morning -- they didn't have that before. Life is still hard, but now they're free. [Through the newsletter] I wanted to let people know that the soldiers and civilian contractors are doing amazing things, and they're making a difference for the people of Iraq."

Anne Pennsy works as the office manager for Shaler dentist Arnold Peace. "[Patients and co-workers] ask me about him all the time, and they've all read the newsletter," said Pennsy. "But when I read those newsletters, I look at them more for the English, and I'm so proud of the way he writes.

"He was so descriptive when he wrote about bringing back the 900th soldier killed [in the war]. I could tell how he felt when they put that boy on his aircraft, and I thought to myself, 'Paul, find out who that kid is,' which he did," recalled Pennsy. "Once he wrote about picking up a member of the marching band, and one kid forgot his drum. Paul was frustrated because he had to stay on the ground longer than he was supposed to, which was dangerous. I understand the emotion when he's writing."

She added that she also understands his career as a soldier when he explains it in terms of her own job. "When I asked him what a warrant officer is, he said, "Arnie's the dentist, you're the office manager, and then there are the hygienists. I'm a hygienist. I'm the techie."

Peace and his wife, attorney Nora Peace, live in McCandless and are Shaler Rotary members. "Before Paul even left for Iraq, Anne promised that he'd speak to our Rotary," recalled Nora Peace. "Arnie is a past president, and one of their jobs is to make sure we have speakers like Paul who exemplify what Rotary stands for, which is service before self."

Anticipating Sherry's eventual visit, several Rotary members received the emailed newsletters. Peace even passed it on to her sons, who are away at college. "Those newsletters were therapeutic and helped me to understand what the conflict is all about," she noted. "I shared them with my three older sons, who are the same age as those who are serving in Iraq, to give them a perspective of what war is all about."

Sherry left Pittsburgh yesterday, after a nearly two-month long furlough, to return to his post in Germany before heading back into Iraq. He commented that being back in America makes him feel as though he had spent the past year on Mars. "I've gotten so used to hearing mortar fire that I jump every time I hear a loud noise outside," said Sherry. "It's nice being here, because there's nobody shooting at you."

A career soldier, he added that his job in Iraq is dangerous but important. "Before missions, you almost have to come to terms with your life every single day, and this makes you take a good look at yourself.

"But like the Rotary, it's a service I'm performing; it's just in a different way," Sherry noted. "Initially we do it to make ourselves feel good, but inevitably we do good."

July 9, 2005

DR. NAIMUR RAHMAN FAROOQI

WHEN HISTORIAN DR. NAIMUR RAHMAN FAROOQI, chair of the Department of Medieval and Modern History at the University of Allahabad in India, was preparing to travel to the University of Pittsburgh in April of 2004 as part of the Fulbright Visiting Specialists Program, he was told to expect trouble.

"When I came [to Pittsburgh], I was given to understand there were anti-Islamic feelings after 9/11," Farooqi recalled. "In fact, I was warned that if there should be an incident, it could be quite hostile. But nothing like that happened."

During his six-week stay, Farooqi, 54, was pleasantly surprised by the welcoming attitude of everyone he met and the large turn-outs for his many lectures in and around the Pittsburgh area. "The students were unexpectedly receptive and interested in what I was talking about," he said. "They also put very good questions to me, and I had a very rewarding experience."

Hosting Farooqi's stay was Dr. Richard Cohen, Associate Director of the University of Pittsburgh's Asian Studies Center. "In response to the 9/11 disaster, the U.S. State Department created [this] program to provide direct access to the Muslim world," explained Cohen, noting that cultural exchange promotes greater understanding, which will ultimately lead to peace.

Farooqi and Cohen acknowledged that the majority of Americans have a negative view of Islam and Muslims, and most universities lack the faculty and curriculum to teach its truths.

"There are very weird ideas out there and stereotypical thinking," said Cohen, noting that Farooqi's visit injected information, awareness, and enthusiasm about this little-known subject. "He was able to [address] a wide variety of questions about the Islamic world. He always wore a suit and had a good sense of self-worth and pride, which was all very important, and clearly made a good impression."

Farooqi, of Allahabad, India, holds a doctorate from the University of Wisconsin and is currently writing about Sufism -- Islamic mysticism -- in India. He team-taught several courses while he was at the University of Pittsburgh, including Introduction to Islamic Civilization, Islamic Law and Society, and Indian Religion. He also lectured to classes and the public at six colleges and universities in Western Pennsylvania and talked about the current political situation in South Asia on radio station KQV.

The world's negative perception of this multi-dimensional and complex religion is perpetuated through ignorance of the fact that medieval Islamists, most notably the Muslim-ruled Mughal Dynasty (1526 to 1858), were secular people who had respect for all religions.

"[The Mughals] were Muslims, and the majority of their subjects were Hindus, and they tried to bring the two communities together," explained Farooqi. "They're also known for their architecture, literature, and the kind of paintings and music they've left behind, because these things are a great heritage for mankind. For example, they built the Taj Mahal, which is one of the most well-known buildings in the world today."

Farooqi's visit was a thrill for Dr. Joseph Heim, history and political science professor for California University of Pennsylvania. "Farooqi's made it clear that some of Islam's greatest governments have actually worked -- particularly in how they related to the rest of the world -- and that's valuable," said Heim.

"Islam is a religion which spreads a message of peace and universal respect for other religions," said Farooqi. "Unfortunately, people in the world today see Islam only as Taliban and Al Qaida. But they are not Islam; Islam is so much more than that."

August 8, 2005

BE SOMEBODY'S HERO

YOU SURELY REMEMBER WHAT YOU WERE DOING and where you were when you heard about the plane crashes on September 11, 2001, but as we approach the fourth anniversary of 9/11, do you know what you can do to remember that day in a positive way?

Here's a great idea: Consider observing 9/11 as a day of voluntary service. That's the goal of relatives of the victims of 9/11, along with business leaders and others who banded together shortly after the terrorist attacks to form One Day's Pay. This is a non-profit group working to establish 9/11 as a national day of voluntary service, charity and compassion. It is not affiliated with any particular charity or organization; its mission is to support all worthy causes.

Over the past three years, One Day's Pay has urged Americans to honor the victims and heroes of 9/11 by setting aside time on or around September 11 each year to perform an act of community service. Last year, nearly one million Americans took part in this grassroots observance, and One Day's Pay hopes to inspire millions more to follow suit as the anniversary rolls around once again.

Says David Paine, co-founder and president of One Day's Pay, "Americans continue to struggle with how to appropriately and meaningfully commemorate the tragedy and pay tribute to those who sacrificed so much on 9/11."

Last October, Congress unanimously passed a resolution asking the president to permanently establish September 11 as a national day of voluntary service, charity and compassion. David notes that the passage of this resolution shows legislators' support in "transforming a day of terror and sadness into a day of generosity and compassion in the spirit of national unity."

It was unity in the face of unspeakable evil that got us through the days and weeks that followed, and every year September 11 serves as a reminder that we're all in this together.

December 13, 2005

WORKING VACATION ON PARRIS ISLAND

IN NOVEMBER, a group of Pennsylvania teachers, school counselors and a few representatives from the news media were invited for an all-expenses-paid, four-day trip to an island -- Parris Island, South Carolina. Think U.S. Marine Corps. Think boot camp.

Parris Island is no vacation for the thousands of young adults who spend 12 weeks at the Marine Corp Recruit Depot learning to become part of one of the world's most elite military organizations. In fact, Marine boot camp is known to be the most challenging basic training program in the U.S. military, physically and mentally.

But don't think Sergeant Carter screaming at Gomer Pyle; times have changed. Discipline is still one of the most important aspects of boot camp, but today's recruits evolve within in a strict but loving brotherhood, designed to raise self-esteem.

In an effort to dispel myths and introduce high school educators -- who will eventually guide their students -- to current Marine Corps training practices, the annual Educator's Workshop is set up as an awareness program that gives a condensed, fly-on-the-wall view of the making of Marines. During the workshop, guests get a close-up look at boot camp training methods and culture by participating in an adventure few civilians will ever experience.

The group from Pennsylvania included educators from around the state, and Pittsburgh's North Hills was represented by Seneca Valley High School history teacher Jim Lucot; Jeff Ritter, associate professor and chair of La Roche College's Communication, Media and Technology Department; and yours truly from North Hills Monthly Magazine.

Upon our arrival, we experienced a recruit's first introduction to a drill instructor and witnessed symbolic gestures; like standing on "yellow footprints," making one last phone call to family and watching chunks of newly-shorn hair fall to the floor.

"There's no access to radio, TV, internet, magazine, newspaper or telephone," Jeff Ritter noted. "Their only contact with the outside world is through letters. But it's not that surprising, because isolation has got to be part of the process of transformation."

The bulk of our time was spent observing and even doing some of the same things recruits do -- including learning to shoot an M-16, going through an obstacle course and eating in the mess hall.

"The M-16 instructional class was outstanding," said Jim Lucot, who was so impressed by some of the corps' educational techniques that he's begun to emulate them in his own classroom. "The Marines teach you so efficiently, and when you left that M-16 class, you knew all the objectives. I've already incorporated some of their techniques. Now I talk about the objective, address it from different angles, and it's outstanding."

Jim is Seneca Valley High School's Selective Service representative, and students often ask him for advice about joining the military. Now he feels qualified to give it. "A lot of kids are real nervous; there's a lot of misinformation out there."

Jim was surprised by how positive the recruit experience appears to be. "I also found it to be more mental than physical and very well-organized," he added. "I think [joining the Marines] is applicable to a certain group of kids and would benefit them greatly."

Throughout the week, we watched as wet-behind-the-ears youngsters trained to become lethal instruments in the global War on Terrorism. And on our last day there, we witnessed a graduation ceremony. Parris Island turns out nearly 17,000 newly-minted Marines each year.

Since 9/11, getting money for college and learning a trade seem to be less of a motivation in joining the Marines than it used to be; most recruits said that they volunteered out of a desire to protect America and its freedoms.

"[Attending each graduation] grabs me like it's the first time I've seen this," said Colonel Steve Hogg, watching as the graduates were embraced by their families and first looked upon as potential heroes. "It's a humbling experience to me to see these young people who have raised their hands at this time in our nation's history and volunteered to go through the rigors of training to become U.S. Marines."

The colonel gave a good description of a potential Marine. "This is not an easy training regimen. But these young people want discipline, structure, and they want to be part of something bigger than themselves. They come here to explore the limits of their strength, their courage, their endurance, and they find new things within themselves. To welcome them into the fraternity, the brotherhood… it's a special day."

"I was impressed and misty-eyed many times during the trip," said Jeff. "These families and the young people are putting a great trust in the government to make the right decisions, and that's an incredibly profound experience."

January 20, 2006

CITIZEN OF THE WORLD

RETURNING SNIPER FIRE ON THE STREETS OF BAGHDAD with a company of Marines was the last thing U.S. Army reservist Paul Abernathy expected to be doing on March 20, 2003 -- he prefers making peace, not war.

"The [Middle East] is a very delicate region," says Abernathy, a fourth-generation American who has both Syrian and African roots. "We must make sure that U.S. foreign policy is good for that region and has the best interests of everyone in mind."

When he was a child, foreign policy was often a topic of discussion between Paul and his grandfather, a WWII Army veteran who was active in local Arab-American organizations.

"My grandfather gave me an acute awareness of international affairs, foreign policy and how important it all is," says Abernathy, who decided to make a career of it and is currently pursuing his master's degree in Public and International Affairs at the University of Pittsburgh.

Born on an Army base, Abernathy also inherited a strong sense of American duty. "My great-grandparents on my mother's side emigrated to the U.S. from Syria in 1917," he says, noting that in addition to his grandfather's service, his great-grandfather fought in WWI. And his parents welcomed him into the world while they were stationed at Ft. Carson in Colorado. They divorced when he was young, and he was raised by his mother, Denise.

Growing up in Cuddy, Abernathy was a personable kid who made friends easily and excelled as a Boy Scout.

"I wish I had a hundred like him," says Scout Master Norman Miller, who's known Abernathy since he first joined Bridgeville Troop 2 at age 10. "Paul was very competent, paid attention to details and always carried out assignments well. He served in every capacity you can in the troop for seven years, and he was one of the best senior patrol leaders I ever had." In 1996, Abernathy attained the honor of becoming the troop's ninth Eagle Scout.

After graduating from South Fayette High School in 1997, Abernathy attended Wheeling Jesuit University in Wheeling, W. Va. While pursuing his BA degree in International Studies, he went to Syria to study and learned to speak conversational Arabic. He also got a close-up look at Middle Eastern culture. "One of the things that makes it so difficult is that injustices are so evident in that region, Abernathy explains. "Their anger is not just the result of propaganda; they see things that are happening, like poverty and the conflict with Israel, refugee camps and military action.

"In Syria, these [circumstances] cut right across three borders--Lebanon, Israel and Iraq. There's a sense of urgency there, but the governments aren't making things happen and they're trying to suppress any opposition. This leads to an organized opposition in the one place where the government can't interfere, and that's the mosque. That's where the rise of Islamic fundamentalism comes from, because that's the only place the government can't form an opposition."

As a result, religious clerics have become symbols of rebellion. "That's why these people are so willing to give themselves to these clerics," says Abernathy.

Throughout his college career, Abernathy served in the Army Reserves, but he didn't think his relationship with the military would go any further than that. "It felt good to serve my country in some capacity, but I never wanted to go on active duty," he explains.

After graduating from college in 2001, Abernathy soon realized that his goal of someday having an influence on U.S. foreign policy would have to wait until he continued his education. "I was leaning towards doing research as a professor at a university or maybe working in the Foreign Service, something in that capacity where you could help advise in U.S. policy."

Undecided about what his next move would be, he worked at an engineering firm for a year before accepting a position in community development at his old university. And then in January of 2003, Uncle Sam sent him his orders.

"I arrived in Kuwait on February 14, 2003, and we crossed into Iraq the first day of the ground war," he recalls. After a few days, Abernathy's company of 172 men was transferred to join a troop of Marines.

"We joined them in Nasiriyah in the heat of [the battle]," says Abernathy, adding that they came upon a grisly scene of wrecked army vehicles riddled with bullet holes. "That's where Jessica Lynch was captured, and we were about two miles away when it happened. We arrived there before anyone else, but we didn't know anything about the story."

As a combat engineer, Abernathy was trained to perform specific tasks. Interpreting Arabic wasn't one of his duties, but because he was the only one in his company who looked Middle Eastern and knew the language, interacting with the Iraqis often became his responsibility -- and his burden.

"They used me as an impromptu translator, and the situations they asked me translate for were not simple," says Abernathy, who tried his best to represent Americans as caring individuals who wanted to help.

"I did make friends with some of the Iraqis, but we had to be conscious of the fact that a lot of the Iraqis who work for [the Army] also work for the insurgency. You didn't know if they were being friendly or they wanted information, because every Iraqi is a potential double agent."

His ability to talk to the natives got Abernathy into trouble with his comrades. "There were members of my company who viewed me as a traitor, because I was really trying to sort things out."

Despite this negative viewpoint, Abernathy was promoted in Iraq, but he recognized the unwillingness and ignorance of American soldiers to respect local customs as a bad situation made worse. "Having our troops [in Iraq] is a factor of destabilization, because we don't understand what's happening. Iraq is already in a civil war, and we're stuck in the middle of it, and that's the problem. I believe we have to leave Iraq.

"Less than one percent of people there are terrorists, but just to be clear, I should make a distinction between terrorists who attack civilians and insurgents who attack only military and para-military. The insurgents in Iraq are mostly Iraqi (90-95%), not foreign fighters like usually played up in the news. The support for attacks against U.S. military is higher," says Abernathy, pointing to a Syrian television show that portrays the ways terrorists hijack the minds of young people and make them do evil things. "That's the perspective of the vast majority of the people in the Middle East, but when they try to talk, we don't listen. We don't listen to anything but violence."

Intent on eventually helping to make this situation better, Abernathy will apply to Ph.D. programs after he graduates in April. And last summer he returned to Syria to research the plight of Christian Iraqis who are being forced to flee their homelands. Says Abernathy, "I'm committed to helping U.S. policy in that region."

May 31, 2012

AMERICAN LEGION POST RENAMED FOR FALLEN HERO

AFTER THIS PAST MEMORIAL DAY, no one in the Laurel Gardens neighborhood of Ross Township will ever forget that Sgt. Joseph D. Caskey went to North Hills High School right down the street. His name and likeness are now memorialized on a large sign that hangs over the Sixth Street entrance of the newly renamed Sgt. Joseph D. Caskey American Legion Post 80.

According to Bob Fleischel, commander of Post 80, the renaming of an American Legion post is a very significant event. "We're rededicating the post in honor of a fallen Marine. It's historical and earth-shaking and heart-pounding for me and all the other members of the military," he said just before the event.

A West View native and 2004 graduate of North Hills High School, Sgt. Caskey, 24, was the commander of his 50-member convoy in Helmand Province, Afghanistan, when the vehicle he was in was hit by an improvised explosive device (IED) on June 26, 2010. This was his second tour of duty. Sgt. Caskey also served in Iraq in 2008.

Rededicating the post in honor of a young man is out of the ordinary, noted Mr. Fleischel, 66, of Shaler. "Bureaucracies usually wait, but we just elected to go with a younger veteran. This was a monumental decision," he said.

"When [Sgt. Caskey] died and his remains came back for his funeral, the reception of the community was overwhelming!" recalled Mr. Fleischel. "This made us see that honoring him as a young man of the community who made the ultimate sacrifice was the right decision. The Caskeys are a military family, going all the way back to WWI."

Despite the sweltering heat, a large group of nearly 400 people, including the Ross Township Police Color Guard, the Three Rivers Marine Corps League, and the Active Duty Marine Color Guard and Rifle Teams, listened to friends, family and comrades give personal accounts of Sgt. Caskey's life and death and the effect he had upon everyone he'd ever met.

"They called him the German Giant," said Captain William Pendergast, USMC. "All kinds of legends are told about him now; how he could throw a football a quarter-mile, best looking man in the world... His magnetism compelled others to follow him, and his strength inspired others to make themselves strong."

U.S. Air Force Technical Sgt. Jeremy Caskey, 34, recounted all the times he and his brothers would pass the American Legion Post on their way to school. "We never could have dreamed that this would happen," he said of the post being renamed after his younger brother.

Marine Staff Sgt. Joshua Caskey, 31, suffered a traumatic brain injury from a suicide bomber during his service in Iraq and is now retired. He talked about how he feared for his brother's safety, especially after Joe embarked on his second tour of duty. "I worried every single night that he was over there that he may not come home," said Joshua, adding that seeing the Caskey name on the American Legion post is an honor and a privilege. "My brother laid down his life for this country, and I am damn proud of that, because this is the greatest country in the world!"

"The biggest thing about today is that we're overwhelmed by the support we're getting from not just our friends, but from people we don't even know who are a part of this community," said Sgt. Caskey's father, Rev. Gerald Caskey. "We're basking in the sunlight of their compassion.

"It soothes the wound regarding our loss, but every time we drive by there, we'll see his name and what it represents," he added. "This is a powerful reminder of a person willing to give his life for what he believed in. We're so grateful for the kindness of the people here in the North Hills, and we know we're not the only ones. Our hearts go out to any family that has had to live with this and go through it. However, the circumstances under which he died were honorable and heroic, and it makes somewhat of a difference to know that his death wasn't senseless."

High school buddy Josh Trembulak, 25, of McCandless, said that the sign gives him comfort. "It will be nice to drive past here and see it," said Mr. Trembulak, noting that he and his fiancé, Stephanie Shola, 24, plan on taking a picture of themselves beneath the sign on June 2; their wedding day. "Joe introduced us."

Sgt. Caskey's girlfriend, Megan Clark, 25, of West View, will continue to honor his memory with the Second Annual Fearless 5K, which will take place at North Park's Boathouse on June 30, 8:30 a.m. Proceeds from the race benefit The Injured Marine Semper Fi Fund. Last year's event attracted more than 700 participants and raised $10,000.

"We're expecting an even bigger response this year," said Ms. Clark, founder of the event, which will feature family-friendly activities, vendors, raffles and prizes. "The message of the race is about taking something bad and turning it into something good. That was the message of Joe's funeral, and I think it's a good general philosophy."

"We need to respect these guys for what they did and what they continue to do for our country," said Mr. Fleischel. "The American Legion is made up of all members of the armed forces, and every family is touched by someone in the military somewhere along their lineage."

Editor's note: As of publication, visit their Facebook page for more information about The Fearless 5K.

March 14, 2014

HOMES FOR HEROES

LOCAL HEROES ARE EVERYWHERE. They are our teachers, police officers, fire fighters, health care workers, military personnel and first responders -- as well our neighbors, friends and family -- and we owe them a debt of gratitude. Senior loan consultant George Payne of Federated Mortgage Corporation in Pittsburgh has found his own way of expressing his gratitude to such people through a national organization called Homes for Heroes®.

According to Payne, Homes for Heroes was formed after 9/11 as a way to say thank you to the heroes of our nation. "This program allows me to give back to our local community heroes by giving them discounts and rebates when they buy or sell with an affiliated Homes for Heroes Realtor and lender," he says, noting that he is also involved with other professional affiliates, such as insurance companies, home inspectors, pest inspectors, title companies, stagers, contractors and other local businesses who are willing to give these people special discounts and savings. "This creates a well-rounded savings package for our community heroes, which continues to give back to them even after they close (on the sale or purchase of a home)."

In December, Payne became a lender affiliate with Homes for Heroes, joining Realtor Beverly Koribanic of RE/MAX Realty Brokers. For the past year and a half, Koribanic, who lives in the Aspinwall area, has been donating a portion of her commissions to local heroes and has been recruiting like-minded businesses to join in the Homes for Heroes effort. "Helping those who serve our country is the primary goal," she says, adding that she also considers anyone who helps animals to be a local hero as well. "I will help people who work with any animal-related organizations, including Animal Friends, the Humane Society, etc. Animals also helped find people on 9/11."

Koribanic acknowledges that buying or selling a home can be stressful. "The objective is to make the buying/selling experience a pleasurable one," she points out, noting that it also helps her business to promote such good will. "But the best part is helping these people, because the look on their faces when closing day happens is unsurpassed."

Payne notes that the Homes for Heroes program doesn't stop at providing discounts. "We also offer the Homes for Heroes Foundation, a public 501(c)(3) charity which provides or coordinates financial assistance and housing resources to those heroes who demonstrate neediness. People don't realize that this program is out there and how many people we can serve with it."

In their efforts to get the word out, Payne and Koribanic have begun addressing groups of police and firemen. "Other than word of mouth, we get a lot of people who go to the website, and if they're in our area, we get an email that someone inquired. We're also looking to speak to organizations for doctors, nurses, and teachers, so we can explain the program to them," says Payne.

Through his knowledge and expertise, Payne can help heroes see significant savings on their closing costs or discount lending fees on purchases. "It's all done within federal guide lines," he says, adding that there is no cost to heroes who participate in the program. "There are no extra fees, no additional paperwork, and nothing they have to do, other than the usual buy and sell of a home."

With his business built on referrals, Payne acknowledges, "You have to show people that you care about them, which is the reason I'm still working. This program is a great fit for me, because it's about helping people."

For more information about Homes for Heroes or the foundation, visit their website at www.homesforheroes.com

Editor's note: As of publication, the website is still active.

April 3, 2014

VETERANS NEED HEALING

THE REV. PAUL BECKER JR.'S FATHER IS A VETERAN, and his son is currently stationed in Afghanistan with the 82nd Airborne. "My regard for those who have gone into battle is high," the pastor said during a special veterans' healing service on Sunday, March 30th at Memorial Park Church in McCandless. Speaking for Allegheny County's 100,000 veterans, Rev. Becker beseeched his congregants and members of the community to reach out and understand the plight of the returning soldier. "We have an obligation to those who have been sent in our nation's name to endure such experiences."

Last year at this time, the "Field of Flags" traveling memorial exhibit took over the lawn in front of Memorial Park Church, at the corner of Duncan Avenue and Peebles Road. The event was so successful in its mission to let the public honor those who have given their lives in the name of our nation that church members decided to follow up with another community-wide call to action.

"The Field of Flags inspired an outpouring of God's love that washed over grieving families, veterans and people from the community," said Jaime Dean, director of Community Care for Military. Mrs. Dean, 48, of Marshall founded CCM while her son, Jarret, was deployed in Afghanistan in 2011. She also serves as Memorial Park Church's director of small groups.

Prior to Sunday's service, Mrs. Dean asked people who have been affected by the "warrior's experience" to participate in a presentation which was designed to help describe the returning soldiers' grief and experience as a platform for their need for spiritual healing and understanding.

The Rev. Becker also illustrated the immediacy and importance of responding to today's returning warriors in a preview of the film "Project 22," which highlights the fact that approximately 22 veterans take their own lives each day. This statistic came from a 2012 study released by the Veterans Administration, which revealed that at least 8,000 veterans a year commit suicide.

Twenty members of Memorial Park Church are currently serving overseas, the Rev. Becker noted. "Our vets coming off the battlefield now have difficulty finding work," he said, adding that thirty percent of them have a disability. "They feel anonymous, and it's difficult for them to relate to people, but so much hope can be offered."

Stephanie Grimes, 29, of Oakmont and Amy Barnes, 31, of Penn Hills both have husbands who have returned from the battlefield with visible and invisible scars. "The community needs to look at them as an asset, not a burden," urged Mrs. Grimes, noting that former military are resilient and have gone through experiences that civilians could benefit from. "They can make our community a better place."

Both women acknowledged that most military members suffer from post-traumatic stress disorder, but this should not define them. "When they come back, they have to re-adapt to civilian life," explained Mrs. Barnes, noting that security and police-type jobs are not a good fit. "They excel at management; have great communication and leadership skills; they're good at time management, conflict resolution, and they all have a strong work ethic. But being in the military is a lifestyle, and you have to redefine yourself when you leave it."

With suicide as the number-two killer of veterans, it's not enough to simply thank military members for their service. "We're less than one percent of the public," said Lt. Col. Tom Stokes, of Shaler. He served as a social worker when he was stationed in Afghanistan from 2010 to 2011. "But we're here, and we need more than just thanks. We need to connect with our community. Engage us, get to know us, learn about what we've been through. Sit down and have a conversation with us. This will go a long way towards preventing problems."

SAVE

October 31, 2014

The 9/11 Memorial Museum

Where were you on 9/11? This question conjures up memories of a beautiful morning that went from bad to worse to the extreme edges of a nightmare. Every one of us was affected, and every one of us has a unique story to tell about the day the world came crashing down and changed our country forever.

I used to live on Staten Island with my brother. Our apartment was perched on the edge of Upper New York Bay, and I had the most incredible view of the Statue of Liberty's armpit and the famous pre-9/11 Manhattan skyline from my bedroom window. I remember walking around the World Trade Center as I hiked down Seventh Avenue towards Battery Park after working on 42nd Street all day in a television studio. I used to stare up at the towering shafts of steel, almost dizzy at the power that was contained within.

I'll never forget skipping along the top of Tower One with Cousin Gary on a summer night in 1989, disappointed that we couldn't look over the edge.

Six months after the attack, I visited Ground Zero and walked along the perimeter of the site with my brother; he had been working in a building not far from the trade center at the time and was an eye-witness. Makeshift memorials were everywhere in Lower Manhattan, and two high-powered beams of light reached towards Heaven from where the Twin Towers had been.

Today the National September 11 Memorial Museum stands in the shadow of the new 104-story One World Trade Center, a.k.a. Freedom Tower. I decided to visit the site again and see the new museum this past summer. It wasn't that I wanted to go there; I felt compelled.

Upon entering the area, the first thing you see are the two acre-sized Memorial reflecting pools. Aptly titled Reflecting Absence, by architect Michael Arad and landscape architect Peter Walker, water falls away into nothingness, and the names of the 2,983 victims of the September 11, 2001, and February 26, 1993, terrorist attacks are inscribed in the bronze panels that line all four sides of both pools.

Since it officially opened to the public on May 15th, 2014, more than one million people have come from all over the country and the world to pay their respects to the victims. Remembrances of the nearly 3,000 people who lost their lives that day are contained within walls that used to rise to the sky; now they speak out from the former building's basement. Literally.

Standing in front of the original slurry wall that still holds back the Hudson River and stopped an even greater disaster, the immense weight of what happened is staggering. But it's nothing compared to the pictures and voices that call out from all corners of the memorial. Suddenly, there's the realization that these people were just like us. One moment they were starting their work day, and then hours later they were pulverized to dust. But here they live on in pictures and words.

The words "historic artifacts" are used to refer to items like the Vesey Street stair remnant known as the Survivors' Stairs, which survivors

took to escape the buildings; the twisted steel that holds the shape of an airplane nose; two crushed FDNY fire trucks; and the "Last Column," a 37-foot-high beam covered in graffiti that was the final piece of steel removed from the site.

However, the reality of the worst terrorist event on American soil is far too fresh in my mind to think of it in such ancient terms. Those items bear witness, but it's nothing next to the stories of the people who died—and the rest of us who didn't. If you want a real, live account of the World Trade Center attack, just go out on the street and talk to the New Yorkers themselves. In my limited experience, it looks like many of them have no interest in visiting the memorial. "Why should I?" one woman asked rhetorically. "I lived through it."

What touched me the most was an interactive digital guestbook where visitors hand-write notes onto a touchscreen. The

notes appear within 30 seconds, overlaid on a world map projected onto a 24-foot screen. The messages appear before your eyes, written by the people around you.

The museum is a melancholy place, but out on the streets of Manhattan in the heat of a mid-summer day, it becomes clear that the faces you see are the same ones that were lost on 9/11. It could have been any one of them, and tomorrow it could just as easily be me, I thought as I considered those brave first responders who rushed in to save those who were rushing out, thinking I'm going to die, I'm going to die... I remembered the haunting cell phone activity that abruptly ceased as batteries went out and spirits sank.

It took more than six months to clean up the site, find the bodies and try to give them their identities back. It was difficult to think about the years they've since missed out on: the milestones of living loved ones that they would never celebrate. In the 9/11 Memorial, they still exist.